FU*K FEAR

A Raw, Honest Guide About Showing Anxiety Who's Boss!

RICHARD KERR

Copyright © 2020 by Richard Kerr

All rights reserved.

No part of this book may be reproduced in any form or by any electronic or mechanical means, including information storage and retrieval systems, without written permission from the author, except for the use of brief quotations in a book review.

First Printing, 2020

Mind Free

ISBN: 978-1-9997864-1-0 Ebook version

ISBN: 978-1-9997864-3-4 Print version

Legal Disclaimer

This book is not intended as a substitute for the medical advice of physicians. The reader should regularly consult a physician in matters relating to his/her health and particularly with respect to any symptoms that may require diagnosis or medical attention.

The information provided in this book is designed to provide helpful information on the subjects discussed. This book is not meant to be used, nor should it be used, to diagnose or treat any medical condition. For diagnosis or treatment of any medical problem, consult your own physician. The publisher and author are not responsible for any specific health or allergy needs that may require medical supervision and are not liable for any damages nor negative consequences from any treatment, action, application or preparation, to any person reading or following the information in this book. This book is sold with the understanding that the publisher is not engaged to render any type of psychological, medical, legal, or any other kind of professional advice.

Any recommendations described within should be tried only under the guidance of a licensed health-care practitioner. The author and publisher assume no responsibility for any outcome of the use of this book in self treatment or under the care of a licensed practitioner.

It's time we showed anxiety
who's boss! :)

Contents

More than just a book	1
You are amazing	2
Have hope	4
So, what's in this book?	7

Part 1
Becoming Fearful

1. My story	13
2. What's going on?	19
3. Am I mad?	21
4. Avoidance	25
5. Lonely	30
6. Fake me	33
7. Distraction	38
8. Telling someone	42
9. The gap	44
10. Rock bottom	47
11. Taking ownership	51
12. Half living	56

Part 2
Fu*k Fear

13. Day 1: Ending the war	61
14. First try	74
15. Fu*k it!	77
16. Riding the wave	82
17. Bringing it home	86
18. Day 2: The Fu*k Fear Technique	91
19. Day 3: Use your Focus	102
20. Day 4: Embrace Duality	105
21. Day 5: Drop the fantasy	109

22. Day 6: Bring yourself home   115
23. Day 7: Embrace your humanity   119
24. Day 8: Forgive yourself   122
25. Day 9: Struggling to bring home   124
26. Day 10: Bringing the catastrophe home   130
27. Day 11: Stop Looking for it   132
28. Day 12: Get bored of anxiety   134
29. Three weeks later…   138
30. Getting married   139
31. F.A.Q's   141

Part 3
Moving Forward

32. Step outside your comfort zone   149
33. Stepping off the gas   155
34. Fu*k setbacks!   162
35. Fu*k worry!   165
36. Increase your resilience   171
37. Quick fixes   175
38. Where am I now?   177
39. Now it's your turn…   179

The online experience   181
A small favor?   182
Connect with Richard   183

Notes   185

MORE THAN JUST A BOOK

———

To help support your journey I've created some helpful tools to compliment this book.

To access them, simply go to https://ffear.co

You will get access to:

- The Fu*k Fear SOS Audio (great for when you need a quick fix)
- The Fu*k Fear Guided Meditation (to embed the core ideas of the book into your subconscious).
- My Fu*k Fear Newsletter full of tips and insights.

Access the support tools here: https://ffear.co

YOU ARE AMAZING

———

You are amazing.

You are absolutely, wonderfully amazing.

You're the pinnacle of 13.8 billion years of evolution. You're a biological marvel of such fantastic complexity that scientists are only beginning to scratch the surface of how you work. Your eyes, your ears, your nose, your mouth, your touch all offer an infinite number of ways of experiencing, exploring and interacting with this mysterious marvel that we call life.

Love, hugs, touch, tears, laughter, heartaches and heartbreaks, connections, journeys, experiences, stories, adventures… Life is everywhere. It surrounds us and it's all here for the taking, to be embraced in all of its wonderful glory. But if you struggle with fear and anxiety, you can't embrace it.

Fear has many forms: dread, worry, panic, insecurity, anxiety, shyness and much, much more. Nevertheless, they all have the same effect on your life — *they hold you back from it*.

I suffered with a crippling sense of fear and anxiety for close to 10 years. It completely destroyed me. Everything crumbled in its path. My confidence, my self-esteem, my social life, my happiness, my sense of freedom, my ability to function as a normal human being. Like a wrecking ball ploughing into a building, anxiety can shatter a perfectly happy life to pieces in an instant.

If you've experienced any form of anxiety, you're familiar with its emotional impact. You feel powerless against its destructive force. You try to fight back, but anxiety is always stronger. You try to run away, but anxiety finds you. You try to plead with it, "Please, stop, please, leave me alone… Please…" But it doesn't heed logic or reason. It's cold, it's brutal and it has no pity.

You try to protect yourself, so you box yourself in and batten down the hatches. You step back from life, play it safe and stick to your comfort zone.

You start approaching everything with an attitude of concern and apprehension. You close your heart and mind to anything different or new.

Social gatherings are missed, invitations are declined, travel plans are scrapped, opportunities are ignored. You avoid anything that's uncertain or can't be controlled — which turns out to be almost *everything*.

Each time anxiety wins, a small part of you dies. You feel weaker. Your fear of anxiety increases. Your life shrinks. Your world keeps getting smaller as, slowly but surely, you become a prisoner of your own making.

You compare yourself to those around you and despise what you've become. You feel unworthy of love. You know that this isn't the life you're supposed to live. When you were a child, you were curious, adventurous, playful. You'd sing in public without a care in the world. Life held so much excitement, adventure, possibility and potential.

But now... Now you're stuck in a quagmire of worry, doubt, shame, guilt, fear and self-loathing.

Sometimes you catch yourself dreaming of being adventurous and bold again, of loving without fear, of embracing all that life has to offer. That's why it hurts so much. You desperately want to come alive again, but you can't. You don't know how to. Anxiety and fear have you trapped, and they're suffocating the life and soul out of you.

And the hardest part of it all is that you're at a *complete loss* as to what you can do about it.

HAVE HOPE

Hope.

It's a powerful word.

If you suffer from anxiety or if fear has impacted your life in any way, I want to make one thing absolutely clear: you *can* get over this. You're *not* doomed to suffer for the rest of your life. Anxiety can be cured, and you *can* be free again. **You can have hope.**

I do not say these words lightly. I say these words because I've experienced the power of hope firsthand.

The type of anxiety I had is known as Generalized Anxiety Disorder, or GAD. GAD is characterized by feeling anxious pretty much all the time — for no apparent reason. It's surprisingly common and millions of people all over the world are affected by it.

My anxiety kicked in when I was 19, and for the following three years, I was *permanently* anxious. As in, all the time. Every moment of every single day.

Do you know that feeling when you miss a step, you're about to fall and a jolt of panic shoots through your body? That's the way I felt each second of the day. It was brutal, unrelenting misery. Unsurprisingly, my life crumbled in the face of this onslaught. I was absolutely convinced I was losing my mind.

Were there dark days? Yes, many. How could there not be? Nonetheless, the one thing that got me through it all was hope. No matter what, I stubbornly refused to give up.

I'm not going to pretend it was easy. As the years went by and my anxiety continued to erode my life little by little, I struggled to see the light at the end of the tunnel. I thought that I was doomed to suffer this misery for the rest of my days.

At times, it felt like I was hanging off the edge of a cliff by the tips of my fingers. During my darkest times, I doubted if I could hold on any longer. I wondered if it might be easier to just let go and fall. Then, at least, the pain would end. No more anxiety. No more anguish. No more me.

But I didn't. I still held on to hope. Yes, there were moments when I wondered if I was lying to myself. There were times when I asked myself if my belief that in the end, it would all somehow — magically — turn out fine was just a manic, desperate delusion. Perhaps that light at the end of the tunnel was nothing more than a trick of my eyes?

Even though I was riddled with doubt, I continued hoping for the best. In the end, that was what saved me. Hope stopped me from giving up. Hope kept me alive.

Was that hope misplaced? No. Emphatically not. I'm delighted to say that it was fantastically, wonderfully real — more real than I could have ever dreamed possible while in the depths of my anxiety.

Eventually, I discovered a way to break free from that prison. I was 21 when I was at my most anxious. Now my fortieth birthday is approaching. I have a family. I'm married, with a wonderful wife and two beautiful, amazing kids. My home is full of love, noise, energy, life in all of its messy glory. Ups and downs, tears and laughter, plasters over skinned knees and cuddles on the sofa... After all those years of fear and torment, I can finally say that I'm *genuinely* happy.

Anxiety no longer dictates my life. I live on my own terms, teaching yoga and running an online nutritional coaching program. If I want to, I can hold a workshop in front of a large audience — or sit quietly on the sofa and enjoy a warm cup of tea.

Don't get me wrong, it's not all sunshine and rainbows. Like everyone else on the planet, I have bad days too. Nevertheless, I honestly believe that the skills I've acquired while conquering my anxiety have dramatically improved my appreciation and enjoyment of life.

Do I still get anxious? Of course I do, although not very often. Anxiety has stopped being a problem years ago. It's a non-issue. If anything, I enjoy putting myself in anxious situations. It's fun! I'm happy and comfortable in my own skin, so it feels good to explore my vulnerable side.

Anyway, I'm not here to boast. I'm telling you all of this because I want you to know one thing: when I was at my most anxious, this life that I have now was an impossible dream for me. Today it's a reality.

It can be *your* reality too. You can have hope. **You can be free**.

Hopefully, this little book will succeed in guiding you towards that freedom.

SO, WHAT'S IN THIS BOOK?

———

Your life is as good as your psychological health is. You might have wonderful friends, a perfect house, a great career, but if you feel anxious and fearful, you'll still be miserable. Let's take some time to sort this out.

The goal of this book is to help you break free from the shackles of fear and anxiety, and the first step on this journey is understanding how anxiety and fear really work. Even though all of us experience some form of anxiety in our lives, very few of us truly understand it. If we feel fear, an instinctive assumption kicks in that something must be fundamentally wrong. Our knee-jerk reaction is to run away from fear, get rid of it, fight it, hide from it, reject it, deny it. The last thing we want to do is actually look at it and try to *comprehend* it.

Isn't it strange that our lives can be controlled by this powerful, dominant force that we barely even understand?

We naturally fear what we don't understand. A pitch-dark room can be eerie until we flick the light on. Knowledge and understanding shine a bright light on fear. They disperse the darkness and reveal the truth. Once we see our anxiety for what it truly is, we realize that there's nothing to be afraid of and it loses its power over us.

This is not just about a fear of public speaking or a fear of flying. This is about understanding the inner workings of anxiety and fear itself. Once we grasp its nature, we can apply this knowledge to all fear-inducing situations.

To help you gain a true understanding of fear, I'm going to walk you through my personal, first-hand experience with overcoming anxiety. I'll share my raw and honest account of how anxiety destroyed my life and, more importantly, how I discovered my way back to happiness, peace and contentment. I'm going to walk you through each step of my journey and reveal my most valuable insights to you.

This is not your typical anxiety book

We're going to go straight to the trenches and get a nitty-gritty, insider's view of anxiety. This is an important point. Too many anxiety books are written by people who have never gone through it. They don't *really* get it. By sharing with you my personal, messy, painful moments — or, in other words, by revealing the stuff that no one wants to talk about — I want to give you a deeper insight into anxiety and a better understanding of it. It is my hope that reading my story will allow you to get a grasp on the reality of living with anxiety and fear — and for those of you who are already living it, my goal is to let you know that you're not alone and you can break free.

In this book, not only will you learn how to overcome anxiety and fear, but the skills that you acquire along the way will help you rise up and grow as a person. You'll learn to open up to who you are and be okay with that. This book is all about becoming you, *all* of you — not just the parts you aren't afraid to show to the outside world. The ultimate destination is a deep sense of freedom, contentment and connection to the real you.

The *Fu*k Fear* approach is relatively simple. Anyone can do it. That's the thing: because anxiety feels so massive and scary, we convince ourselves that overcoming it must be hard and complicated too. In reality, it doesn't have to be that way at all.

My promise to you is that I'm going to keep it as straightforward and simple as possible. I'm not going to overcomplicate things with fancy jargon or complex multi-step processes. The last thing you need when you're anxious is a checklist of things you must do.

I want to stress that not all of the ideas in this book are originally mine. Although the *Fu*k Fear* approach is based on my personal experience, it also contains elements of acceptance and commitment therapy (ACT), self-compassion therapy, Zen practices that are thousands of years old, and the work of an anxiety expert Barry McDonagh. I'm standing on the shoulders of giants here. Think of me as the glue sticking it all together.

It's also important for me to make it clear that I'm *not* a doctor, a trained psychologist or anyone with professional medical training, nor do I pretend to be. I'm just a normal guy who has suffered from serious anxiety and figured a way out. If you want a doctor's take on anxiety, there are plenty of books out there. This is my take.

As you go through the book, feel free to pick and choose the aspects that resonate most with you. There are no strict rules or guidelines. Trust your gut instinct as to what works best for you. I'm giving you a road map, but you're free to discover your own path to freedom and happiness. The more I can empower you to be the master of your own destiny, the better.

Lastly, before we get stuck in: I know it can be hard to read a book about anxiety. All that focus on it can make you feel, well, anxious. You may feel tempted to put the book aside, hide your head in the sand and wait for your problems to go away by themselves. Sadly, hiding doesn't work. It's a waste of time. Trust me, I wasted far too many years of my life trying to hide from anxiety and fear. So I encourage you to push through the discomfort and stick with it. Eventually, you'll reach all the good stuff that's waiting for you on the other side.

Keep in mind that if you do feel anxious while pursuing the path towards freedom, it's generally a good sign. It means you're stepping outside your comfort zone, trying something new and growing as a person. Besides, you've got me now. I'll be by your side through all of this. We're going to get through it together.

Life is short. Let's not waste any more of it to fear. Let's not be too afraid to *really* live.

A BOOK OF THREE PARTS

Just so you know what you're getting yourself into: this book is divided into three parts. Each part explores a different aspect of anxiety and fear.

Part 1: Becoming Fearful

In Part 1, we gain a deeper understanding of anxiety. How does it work? Why does it feel so intense? How does it hold you back from life? Why do you feel so trapped? We dive deep into my story and use that as an example of how anxiety can tear a life apart. Along the way, I share some of my key insights with you.

(A little note: this part is honest, raw and real. I didn't want to sugar coat it, or short-change anyone who has experienced something similar. Feel free to skip anything that's too intense for you, but know that there's always darkness before the dawn.)

Part 2: Fu*k Fear

Anxiety acts like it's the top dog, but it's not. You are. In Part 2, we show anxiety who's boss. This is all about practical, real-world strategies that actually work. Here we learn how to apply the Fu*k Fear technique to overcome anxiety.

Part 3: Moving Forward

Here's the fun part. Now that you've got a handle on your anxiety, how do you move on with your life? In Part 3, we explore ways to come alive again, be bold and adventurous, and face fears that are still holding you back from life.

PART 1

Becoming Fearful

AKA How anxiety ripped my life apart

MY STORY

I was 19 years old and just a few weeks into my first year at university when it all began. I had finally moved out of home and was excited for the adventures ahead. Hanging around my student house one night, doing nothing in particular, I hopped up a flight of stairs towards my bedroom. As I reached the top, an intense, strange sensation washed over me.

Out of thin air, I felt a wave of fear and dread rush through my body. My stomach collapsed. My skin flushed. My world became heightened and bright. I looked around the bedroom, half-expecting to see a stalker with a hockey mask and a knife. Nope. Just me. I sat down on the bed and tried to compose myself.

What the hell?

Luckily, within a few minutes, the strange sensation passed and my body began to calm down.

That was my first taste of anxiety. A very mild panic attack. Compared to what was about to come, it was just a drop in the ocean.

However, that moment was important for a different reason. Something that hadn't existed before was born. A new little worry box appeared in my mind.

That worry box housed the thought: *What the hell was that awful feeling? I think I best stay vigilant and keep an eye out for any other weird sensations like that.*

The worry box was small at first. You could barely even notice it. So I stuffed it into the furthest corner of my mind and tried to forget about it.

A few days later, I had my second taste of anxiety.

After a Friday night out drinking at the pub, I woke up the next morning to find that something just didn't feel right. It wasn't just the hangover —

although I'm sure it didn't help. This time around, the sensation stayed with me all day. And the next. And the day after that.

I tried to shrug it off, forget about it and just get on with things. I visited my friends and did my best to hang out as usual, but I was unable to relax and let go. I couldn't get lost in conversation or just settle into their company. I felt speedy, impatient, excessively uncomfortable. So I would leave and go somewhere else. When I got there, I would discover I was uncomfortable there too. So I'd move on again.

No matter where I was or what I was doing, I just didn't feel right. I felt like an imposter in my own skin. It was as though my insides were planted into the wrong body and all my neurons, synapses and nerve endings were misfiring. The back of my head felt buzzy and charged, as though it was plugged into an electric socket. My body felt stiff yet ready for action. I had too much energy flowing through my veins and I didn't know where to put it. I would be walking down a safe, tree-lined street on a glorious summer's day, yet I'd feel like I was about to be chased down by a crazed killer.

What is happening?

What's going on?

Why do I feel like this?

Come on, Richy, pull yourself together…

Maybe it's just a blip, I'm sure it will pass, just hang on.

I could chalk up a day or two of feeling strange to a bad hangover, but as the days passed, I began to run out of plausible excuses as to why I could be feeling this way.

Why was I feeling so off?

What did these strange sensations in my body mean?

My worry box was rapidly growing in size and becoming harder to ignore.

I became fearful of how I felt. A part of my mind turned inward and I began to scan my own body constantly, looking for something wrong or even mildly disconcerting.

What's that tight feeling across the back of my shoulders? That's strange, it's kind of stiff!

Why is my head foggier than usual?

Why is my throat feeling lumpy and tight? That can't be normal, can it?

I was on high alert. Like a prairie dog, I was continually scanning the landscape for the smallest sign of any potential danger.

The formula was simple:

Any weird bodily sensations = Danger! It's still here!

No weird bodily sensations = I'm safe. Maybe it's all over and I'm going to be okay.

But I became *too* fearful, too paranoid. Everything started to feel like a threat. Every little sensation, flutter or ill mood was cause for concern. Everything was over-analyzed, scrutinized and judged.

This hackneyed scene is probably familiar to you from some Hollywood thriller or other: someone is hiding in their bedroom closet while a dangerous intruder is sneaking around the house. They're trembling in a heightened state of panic. Every little sound, every creaking floorboard, every moving shadow sends a jolt of fear through their fragile nerves. That was me — only there was no intruder. What left me trembling with fear were my own bodily sensations.

What's that buzzing in the back of my head?! Oh, God! Oh, God! Oh, God! What's happening to me?

Analyzing how my body felt wasn't something I was in the habit of doing before, but now it seemed like it was all I ever did.

I was like a deer caught in the headlights. The fear of strange bodily sensations hijacked my mind and demanded my full attention.

The survival instinct

You see, we're wired to survive at all costs. Evolution has wisely encoded in us an extremely powerful desire to live. It's a fundamental part of our very being, stitched into the fabric of our DNA. We want to live, so we desperately try to avoid anything that might result in death. From an evolutionary standpoint, it makes perfect sense.

However, in order for us to avoid danger, we must first be able to spot it. This is another aspect of our survival instinct: we are ridiculously effective at spotting threats, whether they're real or not. Any kind of danger — a car driving too close, a tiny spider, tense atmosphere or, in my particular case, strange bodily sensations — causes our survival instinct to kick in.

Studies show that a part of our brain is always scanning our environment for any trace of danger (even when we're asleep[1]!). In a sense, human beings are highly-evolved threat detection machines. We're basically smoke detectors with added emotions.

Our survival instinct is extremely powerful. We're programmed to prioritize safety and survival over everything else. Generally, this is a good thing. Our hypersensitive reflexes helped ensure the survival of our species. If they didn't exist, you wouldn't be here right now reading this book. Human beings would have become extinct thousands of years ago.

In a nutshell, the more threatening something is — or appears to be — the more our minds focus on it.

So here I was, in a state of high alert, jumping at shadows, jangling my nerves and keeping myself trapped in a state of continuous anxiety.

I was so focused on my anxious sensations that focusing on anything else became a challenge.

Who cares what's happening in the news?

Who cares about the weather?

Who cares about the amusing incident that my friend encountered on the train home from work today?

It's so laughably trivial.

I'm freaking out over here!

Trying to focus on anything for long periods of time was soon next to impossible.

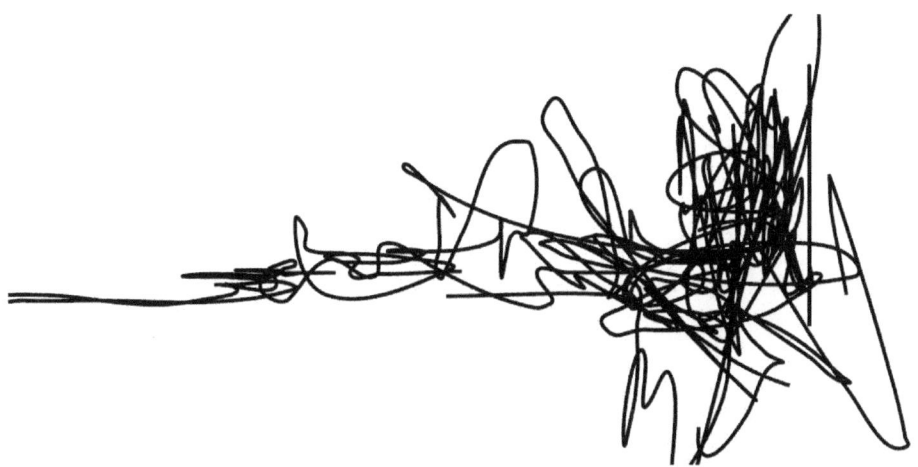

Arrghh! Jesus! What the hell was that?

Oh, no, it's back!

Sorry, what was I writing about?

Anxious feelings don't show up when it's convenient. They pop into your life on their own terms — not yours. Generally, they ambush you when

it's most inconvenient. They like to interrupt the regular flow of your thoughts and

make even the simplest tasks difficult.

 **Key insight**

Anxiety can feel freaky, intense and scary. Anything *perceived* as threatening or dangerous instantly hijacks your attention.

WHAT'S GOING ON?

So why was I so scared of some strange bodily sensations?

Let's give this a bit of context. Let's backtrack a little.

I grew up in a small town in Northern Ireland. As childhoods go, I really can't complain. I was surrounded by a loving, supportive family and had a handful of trustworthy, lifelong friends.

I wasn't really a nervous child. If anything, I was the opposite. I was well-adjusted and reasonably confident for a teenage boy. I might have even been a little bit too cocky for my own good. I had no past traumas and there were no skeletons in my closet. I was happy.

So when I started to feel anxious, I had no clue what was going on. Anxiety was the last thing on my mind. Why would I have been anxious? Life was great! I finally moved away from home, I started attending university, I was making new friends. What could I have possibly been anxious about?

Sure, I had experienced periods of intense worry and stress before. But this felt nothing like worry. This was something *very* different. It was alien, intense and troubling. This new and threatening feeling was so unlike anything I'd ever experienced before that I had no reference point. I was clueless. I just couldn't put two and two together. There was no way for me to know that what I was dealing with was actually anxiety.

Because I couldn't understand what was happening to me, I began to suspect that I was suffering from a severe, life-altering, perhaps irreversible mental health condition.

You see, there's a history of mental illness on both sides of my extended family — grandparents, uncles and cousins included. Growing up, my parents always warned me to be careful and to avoid drugs because our family was at risk of mental health issues.

I know my parents had the best intentions and were just looking out for their kids. But being warned time and time again that I was genetically predisposed to losing my marbles conditioned me to think that this was precisely what was happening to me. I mean, it genuinely *felt* like I was going crazy.

As fears go, the fear that you might be losing your mind is, well, a biggy. Thinking about this, I saw myself locked up in a padded cell, medicated to within an inch of my life, drool dripping down my chin. I know this is a very simplistic, backward and totally inaccurate view of mental healthcare. Mental health services and facilities have advanced massively over the past 50 years. A part of me knew that it didn't really make sense, but that image still stubbornly lodged itself in my brain — and it horrified, terrified and petrified me to my very core.

That image fuelled my anxiety. It poured gasoline on the fire. Every strange bodily sensation was now further evidence that I was losing it. In this heightened state, even the most minor discomfort could lead to a massive meltdown.

 Key insight

> If you don't realize that you're simply anxious, the sensation of anxiety can feel even more fearful and threatening.

AM I MAD?

I'm wide awake. I can't sleep. Outside, I hear birds waking up and beginning to chirp. *Fu*k, is it morning already?!*

All night long, three questions have been spinning in my mind.

What's wrong with me?

Why do I feel this way?

Am I going mad?

Fear drives my thoughts. I'm desperate for an answer.

What's wrong with me?

Why do I feel this way?

Am I going mad?

If I could just make sense of WHAT is happening, then perhaps I'd figure out WHY it's happening to me — and maybe then I'd finally find a solution.

What's wrong with me?

Why do I feel this way?

Am I going mad?

I don't know. God, I hate not knowing! Perhaps I just need to think about it some more?

What's wrong with me?

Why do I feel this way?

Am I going mad?

My mind won't stop interrogating itself. Three questions stuck in a perpetual loop, coming back to me again and again in desperate hope that maybe someday, somehow, I'll figure out what the hell is going on.

What's wrong with me?

Why do I feel this way?

Am I going mad?

Am I going mad?

Am I going mad?

The question hangs in the air with the weight and intensity of an elephant.

Am I going mad?

That's the thing about anxiety: it really *can* make you feel like you're losing your mind. When you're trapped in an anxious state, your perception shifts and your interaction with life changes at a fundamental level.

It's one of the hardest things to get across about anxiety — that radical perception shift. Unless you've experienced it, it's nearly impossible to understand.

You don't just feel off or unwell. It's nothing like being sick with the flu. Even if you catch a particularly bad cold, you're still unmistakably you. You still recognize yourself as a person. In the midst of physical sickness, there can still be pleasantness, niceness, warmth and love. You can still snuggle up on the sofa with a cup of hot chocolate.

But when you're suffering from anxiety, everything doesn't just *feel* off — in your mind, you're certain that it *is* off because that's what your senses are telling you. If your feelings, thoughts and bodily sensations all point towards something being threatening and dangerous, then, for all intents and purposes, it is threatening and dangerous — at least to you.

It's like flicking a switch. Even though your life is exactly the same, what seemed fine and dandy yesterday is suddenly transformed into hellish misery.

It all boils down to how we respond to stimuli. At a fundamental level, humans are simply stimuli-driven animals. You smell coffee and suddenly find yourself craving a cup. You hear a good song on the radio and start singing along unconsciously. You wake up and feel comforted by your partner sleeping next to you. You see the bright, loving eyes of your kids and experience a surge of joy and gratitude.

But if you've got the anxiety filter on, it all becomes disjointed, disconnected and disfigured.

You smell coffee and your stomach drops as you start worrying about global warming. There's music on the radio, but it's too loud, too chirpy, too different from your inner world. You sense your partner lying in bed beside you and you doubt if they genuinely love you. You see the bright, loving eyes of your kids and dash into the kitchen so you can avoid another one of their inane questions.

The anxiety filter affects every little, subtle interaction that you encounter throughout the day. It takes the colors out of all of them. A fresh breeze of wind on your face is cold and annoying. The sight of an old friend on the sidewalk makes you feel panicked, not delighted. You're absolutely convinced that the checkout girl is angry with you because you're bagging your groceries too slowly. Your comfortable, familiar daily routine is now dull, monotonous and grinding.

Everything becomes cold, harsh, overwhelming and stress-inducing. Words like "nice", "cozy", "safe", "snug", "cuddly" drop out of your vocabulary.

The impact that this anxiety filter can have on your life is staggering. Lou Reed once sang, "I do believe you are what you perceive." I couldn't agree more. Your perception *is* your reality. If you no longer perceive and process life in the same way, are you even the same person?...

One thing is certain: you sure as shit don't feel the same.

During periods of particularly intense anxiety, I'd start disconnecting and really spacing out. My head would feel as though it was wrapped in a thick layer of cotton. My perception would take on a sense of both skewed and heightened realism at the same time. My thoughts would acquire an out-of-body dimension. I felt as though I was watching myself think.

One time, while stuck in this state, I went out for a walk to clear my head. I walked to the shop, but when I got there, I couldn't remember half of what I wanted. I walked home feeling confused. It took me hours to realize that I had actually cycled to the shop and left my bike behind.

This is due to a common side effect of anxiety called "derealization". If you've experienced anything like this before, let me assure you that, although scary and disconcerting, it's not dangerous. It's caused by your natural fight-or-flight response, which redirects the blood from your brain to your core so that, for example, if your arms and legs are cut, you won't bleed to death. This diversion leads to light-headedness and — yep, you guessed it — the feeling of derealization.

You're not mad

The good news is that you're not going mad. Although anxiety can make you feel like you're losing your marbles, as someone who has been there, I can assure you that your marbles are fully present and accounted for.

The feelings of derealization and disconnection are merely side effects of your body reacting to stress hormones activated by the fight-or-flight response. If those anxiety hormones were magically flushed out of your system, you would immediately go back to your old self again.

 Key insight

> Anxiety can *REALLY* make you feel like you're losing your mind. You're not — you're just feeling anxious.

AVOIDANCE

It's been a few weeks now and everything is falling apart. Anxiety is unpicking me at the seams. My confidence, self-esteem and self-worth are crumbling at a remarkable rate.

I'm buying groceries. I'm in aisle three, standing in the health and beauty section. I'm searching for a contact lens solution, but all I can see are rows and rows of hair products: hair dyes, hair conditioners, hair shampoos, hair gels, hair waxes, hairsprays, hair extensions, hair this and hair that... I feel like I've been staring at these products for eternity.

"Jesus, where's the contact lens solution?! Is this even the right aisle? Am I going to have to ask someone? I can't see anyone. Do I have to go and find someone to ask? I'm not in the mood for this right now!"

I feel a wave of dread rise up inside me. Adrenaline and cortisol surge through my body, spiking my heart rate and jittering my muscles. Chemical messages storm my brain, warning me of impending danger.

Blood pulsing, breathing heavy, skin clammy, a powerful wave of fear washes over me. The world around me starts fading away. My knees quiver and my ears go deaf. There's a strange feeling in my chest. I can't get enough breath.

Shit. I think I'm having a panic attack.

If you haven't experienced it, you don't know how it feels. But if you have, you know it only too damn well.

I feel my fight-or-flight response kick in. Fight-or-flight? What a joke. Fight? Fight who? There's no one to fight. Flight? Where can I run to? I can't run from myself.

I'm sensing danger everywhere. What kind of danger could possibly be lurking in the shadows at this exact moment? Is the shop attendant going to pull a gun on me? Am I about to have a heart attack? Is the roof going to collapse on my head? Well, none of these are very likely. So why do I feel so afraid?.. I don't know.

I'm obviously safe. The rational part of my mind knows this, yet no matter how much I try to convince myself otherwise, I can't make myself calm down and relax.

Fear doesn't always make sense. It's like when you notice a little spider crawling over your hand. Your nervous system reacts, your heart jumps and your adrenaline spikes. There is no danger. It's just a little, harmless spider, but your fear response is triggered anyway.

This type of irrational fear overrides facts and logic. Common sense is suddenly thrown out the window.

That's why people say things like:

"Of course I know that flying is safer than driving. I'm still not getting on that plane!"

"I know there are no sharks in the water, but I don't care. I'm not going in for a swim!"

"Yes, I'm aware that the elevator can safely carry a maximum of twenty people and the four of us are well under the recommended limit. I'm still taking the stairs!"

Trying to defeat these types of fear with logic is generally a waste of time. When fear feels more real than facts, **the facts don't seem to matter**.

My forehead is beginning to sweat. I feel as though the end of the world is upon me. I look around and see other shoppers casually going about their day. I can't help but envy them. They seem so blissfully unaware.

I wonder if they ever deal with irrational fears.

Do they ever worry that they might fall down that space in the middle of a spiral staircase? Do they ever check to see if there's a murderer behind that shower curtain? Do they ever feel panic when ordering a coffee?

Fear is a dominant force in our lives. There are many things that motivate us, but the most powerful motivator of all is fear. Right now, my fear is motivating me to get the hell out of this store. I need to leave, as in RIGHT NOW! So I put down my shopping basket, turn around, walk briskly out of the shop and vow never to return.

———

Certain situations and circumstances start to trigger an intense fear response inside me and I often have no clear idea why. Sitting in the car. Ordering a coffee. Talking to friends. Being with people. Being left alone.

Just like a flesh wound can leave a physical scar, a fear response can leave a deep scar on your psyche.

Fear is hard to forget. These experiences etch themselves into your brain, along with a mental note to self: *"IF HUMANLY POSSIBLE,* **NEVER DO THAT AGAIN!***"*.

You feel hesitant to revisit the places that remind you of anxiety. It's as though your mind associates the place with the panic and the place itself ends up triggering fear.

So I avoid situations or scenarios that may trigger an anxious response in me as best I can.

Situation: I feel panicked and anxious waiting in a shop checkout line.

Solution: No problem, I'll do my shopping online. I'll probably even save money that way!

As best I can, I try to deny the crushing reality that my life is shrinking and my world keeps getting smaller…

Situation: I feel anxious whilst driving a car.

Solution: No worries, I'll take the bus. Besides, public transport is better for the environment!

…I pathetically try to turn every setback into a positive…

Situation: I feel nervous about making eye contact with people.

Solution: That's alright, I can stare at people's eyebrows. No one will notice!

…Yet each time it gets more and more difficult…

Situation: I feel uncomfortable when I leave the house.

Solution: That's cool. What's the point of going out anyway? I always end up back home eventually!

…Each time anxiety wins I feel weaker for it…

Situation: I feel panicked during a lecture.

Solution: That's fine. I won't go to college. I'll just photocopy everyone else's notes.

…It's a vicious loop. The more I run, the more afraid I feel — and so I run some more…

Situation: I fear rejection.

Solution: Easy! I'll just reject everyone else before they can reject me. Ha ha, I win! Who needs friends anyway? They just get in the way. Besides, I've always seen myself as the cool loner type anyway.

…The longer I avoid the situations that trigger my anxiety, the more my fear of them grows…

Situation: I'm afraid of visiting my parents in case they notice that something's wrong with me.

Solution: Why go home? I've been waiting for years to leave and go to university. It's not like I want to run into my mother's arms, sobbing hysterically, desperate for her unconditional love, affection and support!

…It was all done with the best intentions. The idea was to create a safe bubble, lock myself inside it and live a life free from painful, anxious feelings. In reality, I was creating a prison that *prevented* me from experiencing life. More and more, I was becoming a slave to fear and anxiety.

The Avoidance Trap

avoid situation → feel *temporary* relief → feel **weaker** and more **fearful** of situation → (back to avoid situation)

> **Key insight**
>
> Avoidance is a short term fix, that creates long term issues. Each time you run, you feel weaker. Your fear of anxiety increases. Your life shrinks. You feel more trapped.

LONELY

Anxiety feels lonely. Painfully lonely. Not only does it contract the mind — it contracts the heart as well. When you're anxious, it's a struggle to connect with others. You can't relax in the moment and get lost in conversation. You can't settle into someone else's space and just hang out in their company. Because you can't relax, you feel unable to go deeper than the surface level. And the surface level is shallow and unsatisfying.

I grew up with a handful of close friends. We spent years hanging out together. These were smart, intelligent, funny guys I had deep respect for. Because we were so close, I could instantly tell that they suspected something was off with me. What was I to do?

You can't fake that effortless laughter, that natural, warm banter, that snug feeling of camaraderie. I just wasn't able to connect in that way anymore.

I'd never felt more lonely than when surrounded by a group of my old friends, having drinks together, watching them connect, seeing them laugh at each other's dumb jokes and me, shrinking deeper and deeper into the corner. Quieter and quieter. Hoping no one would notice how horrified and destroyed I felt inside.

...

..

.

Oh, God, I haven't spoken in a while.

...

..

.

I don't know what to say.

...

..

.

Say something! Or they'll know.
They'll know that something's wrong with you.
They'll know that you're a freak!

...

..

.

What are you so scared of?
Just say something!

...

..

.

They're all laughing.
I can do that. I can fake a laugh.
"Ha, ha, ha, ha, ha, ha!"
Well, at least I made some noise.

...

..

.

Girlfriend

I remember visiting my girlfriend one day. We'd only been together for half a year, but the chemistry was great. It was a long-distance relationship and this was the first time I was visiting as the new, anxious me.

I had no idea what to expect. I just hoped that it would all go well. I was in so much pain. I needed to feel the warm, comforting embrace of connection to another human being.

Yet as soon as I got off the bus, I could tell it wasn't working. I awkwardly tried to recapture that special connection between us. I tried to muster forced jollity, a chirpy atmosphere, and pretend everything was great. But it was no use. The chemistry was gone.

That complicated dance of neurons firing in your brain, that delightful sustained dopamine hit... It was all gone. Sure, I had a racing heart, sweaty palms and flushed cheeks. But it wasn't because of feelings of passion.

It was an instant, painful crash. After a few days of awkwardness between us, terrified that she was going to reject me first, I started the conversation and suggested that perhaps we should break up.

To protect myself from the pain of rejection, I rejected her.

What I really meant to say was, "I love you, but there's something wrong with me and I'm not exactly sure what. I just don't feel right. I'm crippled with fear and worry at the moment. Can you help me get the support I need? Will you help me get through this?"

But I didn't.

I didn't know how to.

 Key insight

> Anxiety contracts the heart and makes connection with others challenging.

FAKE ME

Inside, I was full of fear, worry and ugliness. I worried that if anyone saw the real me, they'd feel disgust and judge me unworthy. So I decided to hide from the world. I created a new me, a fake me, based on how I *imagined* a non-anxious version of me would behave, rather than on how I truly felt.

At the very start, I could kind of get away with it. I could remember clearly how I used to act around my friends and family before I became anxious, so I simply replicated that behavior from memory.

Every statement — even a seemingly innocuous one — was poll-tested by a focus group that existed inside my mind.

Is this what a non-anxious Richard would do?

Is this what a confident, happy person would say?

Have I said this before in a social situation and did it work then?

Would this sound normal?

Would this get people to like me more?

When you're so focused on creating a fake persona, you stop noticing other people. You stop listening. You're too worried about what you're going to say next. I was no longer having conversations. Instead, I was performing a full-blown stage show called "Look at How Wonderful I Am! Please Love Me, I'm Not Weird!".

But there was no depth to my persona. It was a shallow, dumbed-down caricature of a human being.

As time passed, the memories of who I was before I became anxious started fading. My reference point became fuzzy.

Is this what a non-anxious Richard would do?

I don't know… Maybe?.. I can't remember!

That's when the shit really hits the fan — once you become so out of touch that you've no idea how a confident, happy version of you would act. You start second-guessing everything, doubting and questioning your every move. Any residual shred of confidence goes walkabout.

Like a sinking ship desperately trying to keep itself afloat, I put pressure on every conversation, every interaction, every opportunity to prove myself worthy of love. If I didn't receive constant reassurance that people liked me, I'd become terrified that they did not. Desperate for a positive response, I'd frantically wrack my brain for anything funny, witty or intelligent to say.

Afterwards, I would replay every social situation in my head. I would wonder endlessly what that person really meant when he said such-and-such. I would scrutinize my performance, analyze it, criticize it. Conversations that other people wouldn't give a second thought to.

How did I do?

Was my performance believable?

Did I act normal?

Was I acceptable enough?

Did anyone guess my dark secret?

If I felt that my performance had been satisfactory, I would feel better about myself — at least for a little while. If I deemed my performance unsatisfactory, however, I would feel myself stepping that much closer to the edge of despair.

My fragile self-esteem became utterly dependent on perceived judgment of others. The critical word here is *perceived*. In reality, I had no idea how they perceived me. How could anyone possibly like a freak like me?

It's funny: I was constantly looking for people to accept me, but the whole time I was rejecting myself.

Getting lost

Eventually, I became a compass in the North Pole — directionless. I had no idea who I was. Out of desperation, I started trying on different personas as if I was trying on a new suit, just to see how they would fit.

For a while, I adopted a persona I called *Noisy Happy*. I noticed that anxiety energy is very similar to the energy of excitement. So I turned my anxiety and fear into the latter. Hey, I'm not anxious! I'm excited! Woohoo!

I was the most excited person in the room.

"Whoa, would you look at that? There's a spider. Ha, ha!"

"Hey, it's Monday morning, how awesome!"

"Aren't we having the BEST time EVER?! I mean, like, *ever*! Woohoo!"

Always excited, always ready to party, everything turned up to eleven.

But I was always a bit too loud, too brash, too noisy — a little off.

I just hoped that no one would look too closely and see the pain underneath.

Invariably, even my excitement energy would burn out and I'd find myself in bed completely exhausted, unable to function, too tired to think. Finally, a moment's peace. If I was lucky, I could sometimes spend the whole day like that.

Just noise

At other times, I would just talk. Just to make noise. Just to have something come out of my mouth. But I wasn't exactly sure *why* I was talking — I just didn't want to be quiet, I suppose. Friends talk to each other, don't they? But I didn't know if there was any sort of point to my incessant blabbering. I was just sort of... talking. Just going on and on about something or other. But at least it was noise. I mean, noise is normal. Normal people make noise. As long as I wasn't quiet. Quiet is weird. Quiet is weak. Quiet means something's wrong with you. We judge the world quite harshly, but we rarely judge noise. We can hide in the noise. And, I guess, it didn't really matter to me that it didn't lead anywhere. It was just *there*. It was just filling the empty space. We don't like empty spaces. Empty spaces are awkward. But then again, maybe I'm making too much noise?.. I don't know. I'm not sure when to stop. Is too much noise weird? Oh, God, I don't know. It might be. Are you judging me now? Do you think my noise is weird? Perhaps you can see that something's wrong with me. God, that would be awful. I don't think I could take it if you thought I was weird. Okay, I'll stop making noise now.

Please accept me

It took a while for the penny to drop but eventually, I realized that the more you acquire by not being real, the less you really have. It's all fake.

I was always *thinking* about who I was rather than just *being* who I was. I was drifting further and further away from the real, spontaneous me. But, again, I didn't know what else to do. I was trapped in the corner, desperately trying to survive in any way I could.

I desperately wanted people to love me. To accept me. To tell me that I'm okay and that everything's going to be alright. Even if they simply *liked* me... That'd be good too. But I couldn't tell if they did. I couldn't feel any warm connections of friendship. My insides were just too anxious to let those feelings in.

Even if they did like me, what would it matter? They only liked a big, stupid, fake version of me. That's not the *real* me.

As you can imagine, interacting with people soon became a painful, mentally exhausting exercise. In the end, it was easier to be alone. Then I wouldn't be so frightened of saying the wrong thing, looking stupid or being rejected. I couldn't take that pain. It hurt too much already.

So I avoided being sociable, declined invitations and didn't pursue friendships. During those rare occasions when I did socialize, I was more terrified than ever because I was so laughably out of practice! Living this way made me feel even more rejected — which was the very thing that I was trying to avoid.

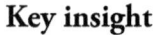 **Key insight**

Resisting who you are and pretending to be someone else is a lot of work that doesn't get you very far. It doesn't matter how much pressure you put on yourself to change or be someone you're not. At the end of the day, you're still just you. You can't run from yourself.

DISTRACTION

I'm sitting in the park. It's a beautiful summer's day. The birds are chirping loudly. An elderly couple on the next bench are carefully unwrapping some sandwiches. There's a young boy running around with his t-shirt pulled up over his head. People are smiling. The air is full of happiness, laughter and light. Yet in my head, it's the apocalypse.

There's fear of losing my mind.

Fear of losing my family.

Fear of losing my friends.

Fear of the future.

Fear of these strange bodily sensations.

Fear that I'll never feel normal again.

I want to run. I want to hide. I want to find a safe corner of the world and just feel comforted, nurtured and cared for.

But how can I run from myself? I can't escape my own thoughts!

Then, suddenly, a light bulb flashes above my head. Ding! Or maybe I can. Perhaps I can distract myself and simply not think about it!

The plan is simple. I'm going set up my whole day in a way that allows me to be too busy, too distracted to think about what's happening to me. If I'm too busy to think, I won't notice how I feel — and then I won't feel afraid and anxious. Richy, you're a genius!

So I keep busy, keep moving and avoid being still at all costs. I fill up my days with work. I make non-urgent chores urgent just to give myself something to do. "Oh my God, I'm running low on spare batteries. Straight to the shops!"

I deliberately repeat inane songs in my head as loudly and as often as I can. *Dale a tu cuerpo alegría Macarena*!

I invent pointless thought exercises to keep my mind permanently busy. "So how would society survive if forced to live on the bottom of the ocean? Mmmmm..."

I get self-righteously angry about trivial stuff just so that I have something to clutter my mental space with. "I can't believe Pluto is no longer a planet!"

Anything will do. I remember walking around Belfast, practicing an impression of Jabba the Hutt from Star Wars: "*Ok Kee La Tee-La Solo!*" I did this for hours. Why? No reason, other than distraction.

Just noise, noise and more noise. It's the equivalent of a child sticking their fingers into their ears and yelling, "LA LA LA LA LA LA LA LA LA LA, I'M NOT LISTENING!"

I contort my thoughts, I airbrush my reality, I lie to myself — all in an effort to block out the massive elephant in the room. Even if it radically distorts my reality, even if my life is a complete lie, I don't care. I'm Mr. Distracted. Mr. Daydreamer. Mr. Fantasy.

Multi-layered

I became multi-layered.

The top layer was fake me: my superficial surface layer, my smokescreen, the "me" I presented to the world, the guy that had everything going for him. "Yes, I'm fine, absolutely fine!" he said with a rictus grin painfully stretched across his taut face.

Below that, a little deeper, underneath that performance, was the second layer. This was all constant distraction, noisy thoughts, busy work, trumpets blaring - think Times Square in New York City on New Year's Eve and you've got the picture.

And then, underneath that endless cacophony... Well, that was where the fear lived. The terrified, frightened, anxious me. Trapped, smothered, drowned out and buried underneath as many layers as I could possibly shovel on top of the bastard. I detested this part of me. He was pathetic, he was scared, he was dysfunctional, he was full of fear, anxiety and dread. He was the opposite of who I'd been before. He was the opposite of who I wanted to be.

In moments of quiet, I would hear him pleading,

OH, GOD! OH, GOD! PLEASE, SOMEONE! ANYONE! <u>HELP</u> ME!!"

I would yell back, "Just **SHUT UP!** Shut up, you miserable asshole! No one wants to listen to your pathetic whining!"

It took a lot of effort, energy and mental gymnastics to drown out that wretched noise.

———

But in the end, it didn't make the slightest difference how much I tried to deny my reality. Reality stubbornly remained the same.

Studies[1] show that we have very little control over our thoughts. Try not to think of a pink elephant. Did one just pop into your head right at this moment? You see, that's just how our minds work.

Distraction can work, but only for small stuff and only for a short while. It's easy to distract yourself from an assignment that needs to be completed or a garage that has to be cleaned — but if you're dealing with something that's potentially more serious, you can't brush it off so easily.

The more I tried to *control* my thoughts, the more *out of control* I felt when these thoughts eventually bubbled up to the surface. In the end, all that constant running from my thoughts just made me more fearful of them.

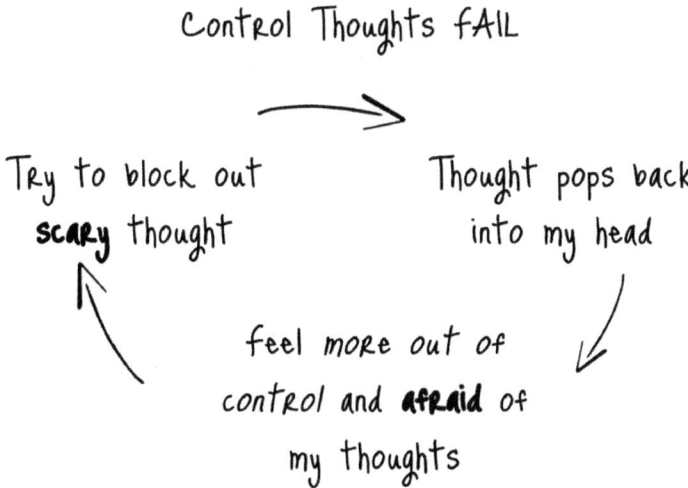

> **Key insight**
>
> Studies show you can't control your thoughts. Distraction works for very small stuff, but not the big stuff. Trying to control your thoughts leads to more tension, stress and, ironically, a greater sense of feeling out of control.

TELLING SOMEONE

―――

It's been five months now.

Five months of nonstop dysfunction, alienation and despair. My life has gone to shit. Nothing feels right anymore. Is this really happening to me?

I realized that I needed help — so I made an appointment to see a doctor.

I explained my symptoms as best as I could. Maybe my description wasn't clear enough, but my doctor couldn't give me a diagnosis. There was no mention of anxiety — she did, however, suggest taking antidepressants. "No, thanks, I'm not depressed," I told her. Well, not yet, anyway.

She explained that she could put me on a waiting list to see a clinical psychologist. Unfortunately, I'd have to wait for at least nine months.

I said, "Okay. That's fine."

But what I really meant to say was, "Nine months! Nine f*%king months! Are you SERIOUS?! I've barely made it through this morning! What am I supposed to do for the next nine months?!?"

On the way out, I quietly asked if there was anything else available in the meantime. "Sorry, not really," she answered. As I walked out the door, I could feel my hope for a quick solution dissolving into thin air.

Afterwards, I resolved to never tell anyone else about my condition.

Why?

I was too scared of judgement. There it was. The simple, honest truth of it.

Deep down, I was afraid of disappointing everyone. I was worried that if I told my friends and family what I was going through, they would treat me differently. They would become uncomfortable in my presence and wouldn't know how to act around me. Perhaps, unintentionally, they would keep me at a distance and treat me with kid gloves.

Also, I didn't want to be labeled as the broken one. The one who failed at life.

"Richy? Oh, yeah, he used to be a great guy! And then it all went wrong."

And, besides, what would I even say? I didn't know what was going on myself.

"Sorry, Mom, I think I'm mentally unwell. My mind just isn't working right. I'm not exactly sure what it is but it's crushing my soul and destroying my life."

I could imagine the look in her eyes. The concern, the heartache, the worry, the burden of it all crashing down on her shoulders... I just couldn't bring myself to do it. The very thought of seeing her like that destroyed me. I couldn't put her through that pain. I'd have hated myself even more for doing that.

If I'm truly honest, I think the biggest reason why I never told anyone was that it would have made it harder to deny. Telling others would have made it more real. It would have turned my feelings into a stated fact. Something concrete, tangible and solid. Something much harder to deny or ignore. And that was too much for me to bear. I couldn't admit that reality. I wasn't ready to accept that truth. It was simply too painful.

By not telling anyone — or even getting a second opinion from a different doctor — I failed to get the support I so desperately needed. Please, don't make that mistake. If you suffer from anxiety or phobias, please, get as much help and support as humanly possible. It turns out that there's a lot of truth to the saying that a problem shared is a problem halved. Talk to a friend, contact your doctor, find a support group, join an online forum. You don't have to carry this burden alone!

 Key insight

Try not to make my mistake of being too ashamed to ask for help. Getting support really helps. Share the load.

THE GAP

My old life was dead. I was no longer who I used to be. That person was gone. More than anything, I desperately wanted my old life back.

My old life became a benchmark, a touchstone, a symbol of my own personal heaven.

I constantly tried to recapture my old life. I relived old memories, thoughts, experiences, and tried to lock them in my mind, as though remembering a feeling or experience clearly enough could somehow make it real again. As though I could remember the old me back into existence.

I'd drift off into daydreams where I was the non-anxious Richard again. I'd imagine delightful scenarios of me just sailing through life and everything being wonderful. I'd imagine myself being super sociable, everyone loving me and laughing at my jokes.

I'd even dream about it — but then these dreams would change and suddenly, I'd be abandoned, lost and alone. Fear would strike me. I'd try to run, but my legs would fail me.

Grief

I didn't realize it at the time, but, in hindsight, I was in the depths of mourning. The grief I felt was profound.

I felt like a part of me had died. My life as I knew it had been savagely, brutally, cruelly ripped away from me. Without notice or warning, without saying goodbye, without anyone else in the world acknowledging the pain it caused me. I felt it. It would hit me in waves and almost floor me. I was heartbroken — or rather heart-*shattered*. I was aching inside and it pained my soul intensely.

Grief isn't just a mood or an emotion. It's a state of being. It refuses to let go of you. It's always there in some shape or form. Some days are better than others, but you can never shake it off completely.

A profound weight now pressed on my shoulders and gripped my stomach. Existence contained an undercurrent of despair and uncertain yearning.

I saw this as a major problem.

By being miserable, I was creating an ever bigger gap between where I was and where I wanted to be. Everything in my life was measured against the non-anxious me — and everything was coming up short.

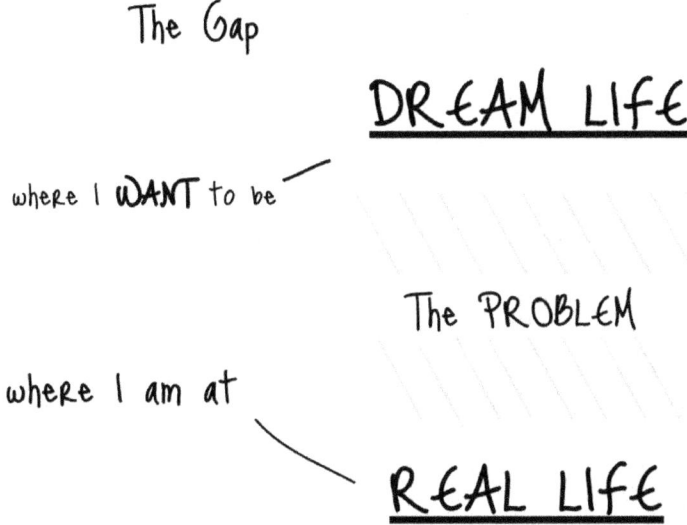

Rather than living the life I had, I was busy comparing everything to how my life was before I became anxious, and constantly being disappointed by the difference.

The thinking was, "IF I'M MISERABLE NOW, I'LL NEVER BE THE HAPPY ME AGAIN!"

It was as if someone was standing next to me, shouting, "You shouldn't be feeling like this! You'll never be the old you again if you're a pathetic sack of sadness!'

I felt grief, despair and anguish because I'd lost the old me — and then I felt angry at myself for feeling that way.

So I didn't allow myself to acknowledge the pain, to feel the grief or to accept that some heavy shit had gone down. Instead, I fell back on my default defense mechanism of denial and attempted to block out and numb the pain in any way I could think of.

More and more, I rejected every aspect of my anxious life. More and more, I fought against being me.

Did it work?

Of course not.

It's not like you can select which emotions to numb. "I think I'll numb my fear and grief today." Nope. When you block out feelings, you block out all of them — including happiness and joy.

To make matters worse, the more I tried to resist the feelings of grief and pain, the more threatened I felt when they did inevitably show up.

In truth, I couldn't have been more cruel to myself if I tried. I would never ignore a child in tears, yet I ignored my own pain. Ignoring my pain only served to make me feel more unloved and unworthy. The eventual conclusion was that *if my pain didn't matter, then* **I didn't matter**.

 Key insights

> As the saying goes, comparison is the thief of joy. Judging your life against a perfect ideal only serves to make you feel more inadequate and miserable.
>
> You wouldn't ignore a child's suffering, so why ignore your own?

ROCK BOTTOM

It was time for my appointment to see the clinical psychologist. I found the message in my mailbox. I opened up the envelope, read the letter and then just threw it straight into the bin. Nope. Not interested.

It's hard to comprehend my motivation here. I was so invested in the fake me, the "everything-is-wonderful" version of me, that I convinced myself I didn't need the appointment. Denial at the highest level. My reality distortion filter was in full effect. My head wasn't just stuck in the sand — my whole body was buried in it.

Without help, I simply stayed trapped in an anxious state. For the next two years, I remained consistently anxious.

My life developed an uncomfortable routine:

> Eat, sleep, be anxious, repeat.
> Eat, sleep, be anxious, repeat.
> Eat, sleep, be anxious, repeat.
> Eat, sleep, be anxious, repeat.
> Eat, sleep, be anxious, repeat.
> Eat, sleep, be anxious, repeat.

To survive, I created a set of rules to help me get through each day.

Richard's Desperate Rules For Surviving Anxiety

1. Avoid all situations or places where you've been anxious before.
2. Stay busy.
3. Stay distracted.
4. Don't commit to anything that you can't get out of at a moment's notice.
5. Always have an excuse ready to escape from any event if needed.

6. Know where the toilets are. (Toilets are an excellent place to freak out. It's normal to leave a room to go to the loo. The door can be locked. Typically, it's just you. I had numerous freakouts in the bathroom only to recompose myself five minutes later and continue on with the facade.)
7. Never work in an office, even part-time. (I learned that the hard way. Office environments and me don't mix.)
8. Avoid getting to know anyone too well. (In case they learn to see through your bullshit facade.)
9. Act like you're having a blast — if you look like you're having a great time, people will be less likely to question your reality.
10. Tell *no one* you're anxious, EVER!

But the more rules I had, the more imprisoned I felt.

As time went on, my energy and motivation dwindled. It was a challenge to get out of bed in the morning. My grades plummeted. I barely attended my university lectures. Even when I was there, my mind was somewhere else. It was a miracle I wasn't expelled.

My social life shrank down to a handful of people who, I hoped, wouldn't judge me too harshly. Mostly, I stayed indoors and avoided the world. I started drinking heavily so I could take a short vacation from being me — and being hungover was a great excuse as to why I wasn't functioning so great. I also began regularly smoking marijuana. (Important side note: marijuana and anxiety DO NOT MIX! Super *not* recommended.)

I knew that in the long run, it really wasn't helping, but at least it gave me an excuse to sit inside all day and do nothing. As far as others were concerned, it helped explain why I was so dysfunctional.

Sometimes I'd try to muster up the courage to step outside my comfort zone and engage with the world, but anxiety would always strike me down. Each time I hit a dead end, I'd sink a little lower. Soon it became too painful to even try. It hurt too much to fail over and over again. Staying down was easier than falling and then trying to get back up again.

Every now and then, I'd find myself yelling up at the heavens, "LIFE IS NOT SUPPOSED TO BE THIS WAY! There has been some sort of mistake! Why did this have to happen to me? What did I do to deserve this?!"

No answer in the deafening silence that followed.

Hope started to dwindle. I began to wonder if I was doomed to suffer for the rest of my life. Depression is the absence of hope, and I was growing increasingly depressed.

I could feel myself drifting into a slump, a fallow state, closing off life and turning off reactivity. I became isolated from everyone and everything. Sure, I was giving up on life, but the trade-off was that I was also dulling the pain. I was tired of hurting. I was tired of feeling afraid all the time. I was just plain tired.

At least by maintaining a low-grade depression, I could shield myself from real unhappiness. If I'm not optimistic, I won't have to fall so hard, right? If I expect to be disappointed, then being disappointed won't be so disappointing. So I chose a dull, grey life.

As time passed, the line between me and my anxiety blurred. I was feeling anxious all the time, so perhaps it meant that my anxiety *was* me?

What would happen if my anxiety left? Who was going to be left behind? Would there be *anyone* left afterwards? Or would it just be a gaping void?

Unsurprisingly, my behavior was becoming more and more erratic. I'd fluctuate between a fallow state and being confrontational, aggressive. I got into a fight with my lecturer. I argued with my family over non-issues. I tried to steal my friend's girlfriend on a drunken night out.

I was aware of the changes in my behavior, but I felt powerless to stop it. There was too much mess, anger, anguish and despair inside my body, and it just kept bubbling up to the surface.

Sometimes I acted erratically and dangerously just to spike my adrenal glands. The strange thing about adrenaline is that it gives you a moment of clarity. It brings life back into sharp focus and makes you feel more alive. If you're trapped in the fog of anxiety and depression, adrenaline can feel like manna from the gods.

To be honest, it's a challenge to remember this time in my life. With my brain only half-engaged, my memory is foggy at best, with large gaps in between.

However, I do remember the dark thoughts that would often flash through my brain.

"No one will ever love a freak like me. I'll die sad and alone."

"You coward! You're just a f**king coward! A yellow coward. Running scared. Afraid of life."

"What's the point anyway? We're all going to die someday."

I remember thinking I'd do anything to feel normal again. I would have happily cut off my legs if it had helped me to get rid of that inescapable, constant anguish. The scary thing is that I was being deadly serious. It would have been a no-brainer. I'd have happily waved my legs goodbye.

A few times, lying in bed alone, wallowing in anguish, I did consider just ending it all. Just doing the final deed. It definitely crossed my mind more than once. A part of me was shocked and horrified that I was thinking that way, yet another part felt tempted by the relief I would have felt. I don't think I ever took it entirely seriously, but I did wonder how much misery I could sustain before I *would* start taking it seriously. Thankfully, something in me refused to give up hope. I refused to let my story end that way.

 Key insights

Without hope that you can get over this, you can become increasingly depressed. You can feel tempted to turn away from life so you can numb your pain.

The good news is that there *is* hope. You can get over this.

Recognize that anxiety can lead to depression and seek medical help if you're at that stage. If you find yourself having suicidal thoughts, please seek help immediately. You can find a comprehensive list of global support lines at www.suicide.org.

TAKING OWNERSHIP

So here I was, at my rock bottom. A hopeless, anxious, broken mess. And then my older sister paid me a visit...

It was late in the afternoon when my sister called round. I was slumped on the sofa, alone, playing computer games in the dark. I wanted her to leave. I didn't feel like speaking to anyone.

She didn't look particularly pleased to see me either.

"Have you sat here all day? Tell me, what exactly have you done today?"

"I went to the shop!" I said smugly, without bothering to take my eyes off the TV screen.

And it was true. I walked all the way to the shop. The shop was literally on the corner of my street. It was a two-minute walk at most. I bought some milk and bread. And I remember actually feeling proud of myself for having achieved that — as though I could wear it as some sort of badge of honor.

I took a moment to turn around and look at her — and then I saw it. A look of concern and worry on her face. As though she was thinking, "What's happened to you, Richy? How can I help you?"

And that was it.

In that brief moment, I saw myself through my sister's eyes with clarity and focus. I thought, "Have I really stooped that low? Is walking to the corner shop really going to be the crowning achievement of my day? Is this my life now?"

I used to do things. I used to be engaged. I used to be someone. I used to be alive!

I felt ashamed. Ashamed of who I'd become, ashamed of how far I'd fallen, ashamed that I'd given up on life.

My sister went into the kitchen to make a pot of tea and I just sat there, dumbfounded, my brain swirling with the reality and truth of that moment.

I realized right then and there that I had to make a choice. I could continue living like this, finish playing that pointless computer game and smoke some weed. I could keep on blaming life, my bad luck and my unfortunate genetic blueprint, stewing in my victimhood, sinking deeper and deeper into despair. A "do-nothing-and-don't-try" kind of attitude.

Or...

I could stop playing the victim card, put down the game controller, get up from the sofa and take ownership of my life. Yes, some heavy shit had gone down. I didn't want it. I didn't cause it. I didn't ask for it, but it was still there. This was my reality. If I didn't accept my reality, I could never move forward with my life. I would remain stuck.

Yes, it was a lousy hand, but it was the hand I'd been dealt. The game wasn't over yet. I could still pick up my cards and give it my best shot.

"So, Richard, will you continue to play the victim? Will you give up and throw in the towel? Or will you dust yourself off, get back up and refuse to let your circumstances dictate who you become?"

Right then and there, I made a choice.

Quietly, without any trumpets, drama or an Oscar-worthy speech, I chose to be fully responsible for my life.

It made sense. At the end of the day, I was the only person who could take that responsibility. Whatever happened, the buck stopped with me. If I didn't own my life, no one would and my life would go to waste. No one else was going to save me. The only person who could *truly* rescue me was... me.

The bottom line was, I may not have been responsible for creating my anxiety or my fear, but I was responsible for how I responded to it now that it *was* here. I was responsible *to* how I felt, rather than *for* how I felt.

And I meant it. I truly meant it, deep down inside, where my truth resided.

It was a silent moment, but it was real and it was all I needed. My suffering was not the end of me. My story would continue.

My sister came back with the tea and we chatted for a bit. After she left, I got up from the sofa and set about reclaiming my life.

Things were never the same after that.

It's not always a big dramatic event that shakes us out of our slump. Sometimes, it's the smallest things that turn everything around. Don't wait for life to send you a glaring, huge signal that things need to change. The small signs are just as valid as the big ones. I don't think it gets much smaller than your sister asking you what you've done that day, but really that can be all that's needed (thanks big sis, love you loads!).

Taking responsibility

This was my first step towards freedom. Taking responsibility for where I was at.

In no way do I want to downplay how challenging living with anxiety is. It's perfectly normal to feel overwhelmed with grief, sadness and pain. It's natural to want to blame your circumstances or your bad luck, but there comes a point when it's more helpful to focus on what you can do about it, rather than what's *wrong* about it. Yes, sometimes life isn't fair, but focusing on suffering won't change anything.

Taking responsibility for your suffering can be a hard pill to swallow — especially when it's not your fault — but let's make one thing absolutely clear: once you own your suffering, an amazing thing happens. It frees you. You're no longer stuck. You're no longer a helpless victim of your circumstances. You can now move forward with your life.

Your energy will no longer be wasted on blame and self-pity. You'll be able to accept your suffering and yet still work on changing it. You'll be able to focus on how to improve your life. You'll be able to decide how you wish to react to what's happening to you. You'll be able to shift your focus and strength towards a much more empowering mindset. You'll be able to ask, "What can I do about it?"

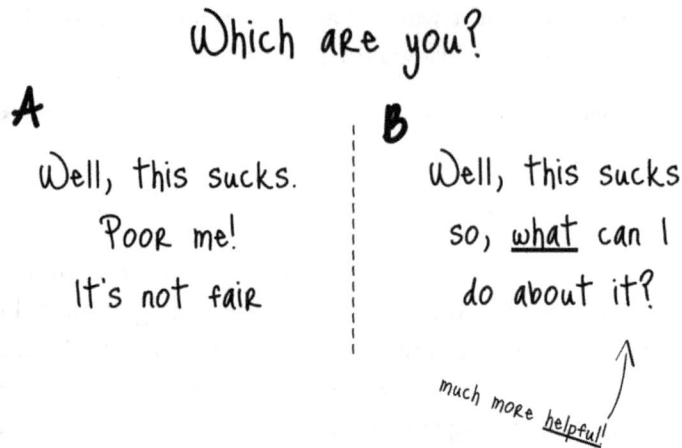

This simple shift helps you reclaim control over your life. It may seem minuscule, but it changes everything.

People like Christopher Reeve, the actor from *Superman*, are an endless source of inspiration to me. Reeve suffered a crippling spinal cord injury during an equestrian competition. Falling from his horse left him quadriplegic, paralyzed from the neck down. Of course, he went through many stages of grief after this loss, but he eventually came to terms with his new reality. He found the strength to persevere and endure in spite of overwhelming obstacles. He began to actively empower and inspire others who have suffered similarly. He started the Reeve Foundation, which helps people living with paralysis and funds innovative medical research in the field. Rather than fighting his new reality, he learned to accept and embrace it. He refused to let his circumstances dictate who he would become and decided to make the most of the hand he'd been dealt. It turns out, he was a real-life Superman after all.

Christopher Reeve managed to achieve all of that while suffering with a condition that couldn't be reversed. Anxiety, on the other hand, is reversible. You *can* free yourself from its clutches.

Key insights

It all boils down to a simple choice. Are you willing to take ownership of where you're at?

You can choose to be responsible for your life at any given moment. You can choose how you wish to respond to your circumstances. You can do that *right now*.

HALF LIVING

I wasn't sure exactly what I needed to do, but I knew that I had to do something.

I stopped smoking weed, cut back on drinking and started jogging. Within 8 weeks, I had taken a gap year from my university studies and was on a plane to Australia. I quite literally turned my life upside down.

In Australia, with a combination of fresh air, exercise, eating better, working care-free jobs and making new friends, my anxiety levels dropped. Not massively, but enough for me to poke my head out of the high-alert state for the first time in two years.

I felt a gentle wave of softness and relaxation flood my body. I gave into it and just allowed my body to release years of built-up tension. For the next few weeks, I spent the majority of my days sleeping. I didn't care. It was so great to be able to relax again!

"Oh my God, relaxation! I can relax! I'd forgotten what it felt like!"

Rest did me wonders. I started to feel more like my old self again. It was like all the neurons in my brain started realigning themselves. I began to feel — and recognize — old emotions and sensations that I hadn't experienced in years. I was coming alive again. I was being plugged back in, coming out of the coma and waking up. It was like a fog was lifted to reveal all these living, vibrant parts of me that I thought I'd lost forever. They were simply trapped underneath all that fear and anxiety.

That was a huge epiphany for me — realizing that I was there all along. I hadn't lost my personality. Yes, I was a lot more cautious, wounded, sensitive and vulnerable, but I was still *me*. I found myself again. What an incredible relief!

Was I free of anxiety? Absolutely not. I was still wracked with anxious sensations, but they were more manageable and less intense. If I was lucky, I could even go a few days feeling pretty normal.

At this level, I could function. I could operate on a day-to-day basis. But it still felt like half-living. I wasn't wholly trapped, but I wasn't exactly free. I felt like I was walking around with a dangerous chimpanzee on my back, ready to pounce on me at any moment.

In truth, I still hadn't gotten to the root cause of the issue. I was stuck in limbo. And that was the way of things for a while — a state of half-living.

True love

After a gap year in Australia, I came back to Belfast to complete my degree. Being semi-functional, I could attend classes, focus on my studies and get by.

I decided to go to a party at my friend's house one evening. It was there that I met a Scottish girl named Ali. We instantly connected. The chemistry was electric. From that moment onwards, we barely left each other's side. As cliché as it sounds, it felt like we were made for each other. I had found my soulmate. With all those love hormones flooding my system, my anxiety seemed to disappear completely.

What absolute heaven!

Unfortunately, a few months later, I had a significant relapse. I decided to open up and confess my dark secret to Ali. She was to be the first person to know about my anxiety (not counting the doctor, of course).

I sat her down and explained my mental state as best I could. Her reply — three simple words — ended up changing my life forever.

"You're just anxious."

"I'm just what?!"

That was how I finally discovered that I was suffering from anxiety. To be completely honest, I still doubted if it was true. I found it hard to believe that anxiety could have really impacted my life so profoundly. Now, in retrospect, I can see that it *was* anxiety all along.

It's strange to think about it now — how absolutely delighted I was to discover that I was simply anxious!

One time, during a particularly bad relapse, I was sitting on the grass in the park on a warm summer's evening, just hugging Ali as tight as I could. No talking. Just hugging. I had one simple thought spinning around and around in my head. "She still loves me. She still loves me, even though I'm an anxious mess."

I'll carry that moment to my grave.

Of course, I asked her to marry me. I was anxious, not an idiot! To my delight, she said yes and then immediately started planning our wedding. Though I was really excited to marry the girl of my dreams, a part of me was terrified. I was barely scraping by each day, and now I had to survive a wedding! But I kept my fears and concerns at bay. Instead, I promised myself to finally overcome this. I was determined not to let Ali down.

 Key insights

Your health matters. Looking after yourself can go a long way to reducing your anxiety (we'll talk more about that later). But it's only a part of the puzzle. To really break free, you need to nurture a new attitude towards anxiety and fear.

PART 2

Fu*k Fear

AKA How I showed anxiety who's boss!

DAY 1: ENDING THE WAR

―――

You're getting married in 30 days and you still haven't got a handle on your anxiety.

I know.

Everyone will be looking at you.

I know.

Everyone who's close to you will be in one room, watching you.

I know.

You're going to fall apart. You're going to be a mess.

I know.

You're going to ruin her big day.

I know.

What are you going to do?

I don't know…

I was getting married soon. The very thought of it was making me anxious. What was I going to do? How was I going to cope? I needed help.

So, after another bad relapse, I went to the doctor and was prescribed anxiety medication. I noticed the effects immediately. They really hit the spot and for the next two weeks, I was the most chilled-out and anxiety-free I'd been in years. It was certainly nice to take a break from anxiety, but at a deeper, much more fundamental level, it didn't feel quite right. The side effects of the medication made me feel as though something important was missing from my persona. My edge, my spark, my sense of humor all felt a little dull.

I marked it down as a useful experiment and decided to go off the meds. I knew I could always get prescribed more if I needed to. It's very important to stress here that there are many valid reasons for taking medication and it can certainly be very helpful in managing some conditions — anxiety included. It's just that I, personally, felt that it wasn't the right thing for me.

However, the next day...

Withdrawal kicked in. The most intense waves of anxiety I'd ever experienced. All that pent-up, suppressed hormones being released in one giant flood. Epic waves of fear swamping me over and over and over again. I was on fire, burning from the inside out.

As my luck would have it, that day I was scheduled to present a website proposal for a potential new (and, what made it even worse, *big*) client. This was a massive opportunity for me: if they decided to accept the contract, it would have been a huge gain for my fledgling web design business. I had to perform. I was clueless as to how I was going to get through the meeting, but I couldn't cancel it — it took months for me to set the meeting up. The pressure was on.

The drive to the meeting felt like I was driving to my doom. I was drifting in and out of a fog of anxiety.

Little did I know it at the time, but that was the day that would change my life forever. On this day, I gained a new, fresh perspective on my anxiety that not only empowered me, but put me on the path to freedom. I'm going to walk you through that day, break it down and spell out some key insights for you. As a little side note, I've embellished this story with some additional insights and concepts that I've encountered over the years, but the main crux of it is pretty much what happened that day.

Let's dive in.

The business meeting

I finally arrive at the office for the meeting. I enter the office, open the door to a small room and the three company directors, waiting for me, turn and stare. I feel their eyes burning into my soul. My body feels like it's made of ice that's beginning to melt. Little pieces of me falling away under unbearable pressure. There's a moment of silence. It feels like an eternity. I wonder if I'm going to spontaneously combust.

"Hello, Richard."

"HELLO!" I yell back — or I think I do. Was that too loud? I feel like I'm talking too loud. My voice is echoing in my ears.

"Would you like a cup of coffee before we start?"

Do I want a cup of coffee? Do I want a cup of coffee??? I don't know! How am I supposed to know? What sort of question is that? Oh my God! Quick, Richard, they're staring at you.

"YES," I reply numbly.

During the meeting, I'm barely aware of anything that's being said. I'm just sitting there, going through surge after surge, wave after wave of consuming anxiety.

"Richard, as I was saying, I think this website needs to have a banner across the top. Perhaps…"

WHOOOOOOSH!

"Something that reflects our companies internal policy structure…"

SHHHWWWOOOOOSSSH!

"Delivered within the next four weeks. Before our annual…"

HSSOOOOWWWSSSHHH!

"What do you think?"

"Richard? What do you think?"

Oh, God! It's my turn to speak.

"YES! THAT'S A GOOD IDEA! I AGREE!"

Jesus, I'm burning up here. How can they not tell? My face is on fire. Why aren't they horrified? Isn't it obvious? Oh, God, here it comes again!

And so it goes on.

95% of me is lost to anxiety. I focus on the 5% that still functions. That 5% is the deeper part of me, above and below my anxiety. I put all my focus, energy and attention on that 5%. I just hope it's enough to pull through.

Finally, the meeting comes to a close. Somehow I've managed to hold it together just long enough to not melt into a puddle on the floor. And, to my surprise, the directors accept the contract and sign on the dotted line. The meeting's been a success!

(*It's fnnuy how you can stlil fctnuion eevn wehn you feel so dycusnftaniol*)

I go straight home, burst through the door, throw my bag to one side and immediately collapse on the living room floor.

I desperately need to feel solid and grounded. Maybe lying on the floor will help. I'm sweating, gasping, exhausted, yet absolutely exhilarated.

I did it!

I did it!

I did it!

I danced with the devil and survived.

How did I do that?!

Amazing!

Yes!

WHOOOOOOSH!

Ha, ha! Fu*k you, anxiety!

Go shove it!

You didn't stop me!

I won!

Do what you want, anxiety.

I've already won the day.

It's your turn now.

Do whatever, I really couldn't care less.

I decide to not let my fear of anxiety spoil my victory. I have no other plans for the day, so there's no pressure to be functional. I *fully allow* myself to be completely dysfunctional. I *let go of all resistance* and let my anxiety do whatever it wishes. It can shout, roar or dance the tango for all I care. I've already won the day!

So I just lie there, savouring my moment of glory, letting my anxious feelings buzz in the background.

5 minutes...

10 minutes...

After some time, I begin to notice that my experience is no longer an unpleasant one. I feel, to my surprise… good. Now that I've stopped caring what my anxiety is doing, I don't really feel that anxious anymore. I feel much more centered, stable and at ease — as though some deep forgotten struggle or tension inside of me is finally softening and being let go of. I've never noticed that tension before. It's only when you finally let go of tension that you realize how tense you've really felt. I wonder how long it's been there. It feels very old.

What's going on here?

By allowing my anxiety to run amok and do whatever, I start to feel less anxious?

If I don't struggle against my anxiety, my anxiety softens?

Really? I've always thought of anxiety as something to be fought against, hated, resisted and denied.

I sit up, realizing that I might be onto something.

I hop on my computer and start googling different terms, all based on ways to relax while suffering with anxiety.

I find a bunch of websites that all show coping strategies. Breathing exercises, meditation… Blah de blah de blah. I've tried those already — a thousand times. They were just temporary band-aids at best.

Eventually, I stumble on a website about the process of accepting anxiety, which sounds like something I've just experienced. It's by a guy called Barry McDonagh. His blog posts really resonate with me. He talks about how the key to breaking free from anxiety is accepting it rather than fighting it (by the way, I strongly recommend checking out Barry McDonagh's work on anxiety, especially his fantastic book *DARE*, which can be found on Amazon). Much of this approach is based on what I've learned from Barry McDonagh's work. This book wouldn't exist if it wasn't for him.

For the next hour or so, I follow the breadcrumb trail of information online. This is what I discover:

 1. When we experience a threatening situation, our fight-or-flight response is triggered.

Okay. I get that. I know the basics. I've been stuck in this bloody fight-or-flight for the past 10 years.

> 2. Although this system was designed by evolution to help us deal with physical attacks, it is activated just as readily by emotional attacks — from ourselves or others.

Interesting... So we have the ability to activate our fight-or-flight response through our own emotions.

The next part, however, was the game changer for me...

> 3. The sensations that this fight-or-flight response produces in our bodies can feel very intense and very uncomfortable. If we feel threatened by or afraid of our fight-or-flight response, we sustain it. Our fear of our fight-or-flight response keeps triggering our fight-or-flight response. We become trapped in a vicious loop.

Wait a second…

I can't stop feeling anxious because I feel anxious about feeling anxious! Really?

I guess it makes sense. When you fight against the fact that you feel anxious, you're adding new feelings of anger, frustration and stress into the pot. This exacerbates your suffering — but more importantly, by struggling against anxiety, you signal to your body that you must be in danger. You convince your body that the threat is real, **which keeps the fight-or-flight hormones flowing**, which keeps you trapped in a fearful and anxious state.

This is especially true during a panic attack.

For me, a panic attack would usually start with a simple bodily sensation. I might notice a slight tingle in the back of my head.

"What's that?! That shouldn't be there!"

Initially, I might not even be sure if the sensation is really there.

"Is it back? I hope it isn't. Please, don't let it be it!"

That's when the alarm bells start blaring. My fight-or-flight response kicks in. Adrenaline and cortisol surge through my body, spiking my heart rate and jittering my muscles.

Once the physical response kicks in, the anxiety and fear become real. They become tangible because, well, from a ***physical standpoint***, they are. There can be no doubt about that now — something is seriously wrong.

"I knew it! It is back! Something's definitely not right here!"

No shit, Sherlock! You've just triggered a massive fight-or-flight response. Now that I think about it, it's kind of ironic that my own misguided self-preservation mechanism would end up convincing me that the imagined threat was real.

The feeling intensifies. More adrenaline, more fear, more dread, more worry…

…which only amplifies the anxiety — which makes me feel more fear, dread and worry…

…which only amplifies the anxiety — which makes me feel more fear, dread and worry…

…which only amplifies the anxiety — which makes me feel more fear, concern and worry…

And down the rabbit hole I go.

Fear triggering more fear.

Worry driving worry.

Stress causing more stress.

A seemingly endless loop where my fear of anxious sensations creates more anxious sensations.

My own reaction to anxiety intensifies and amplifies the very thing I'm getting so upset about. Before I know it, I'm trapped in the cycle of being afraid of being afraid. My fear creates the very thing I fear.

If I'd simply ignored my anxiety when it first appeared, it probably would have dissipated in a few hours or days. However, by responding to fear with even more fear, I kept the anxious feelings coming. It was ***my response to these sensations*** that caused me to become stuck in the anxiety trap.

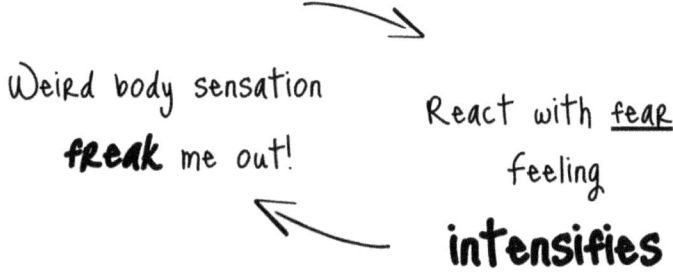

Now, on to the final and most important point:

> 4. The key to breaking free from anxiety **is changing your emotional reaction to it**. You have to **accept your own anxiety and learn to be comfortable with it**. In doing this, you no longer prolong or amplify the fight-or-flight response, so the feelings weaken and dissipate over time.

Is that it?

Is this the key to freedom? I just need to stop resisting my anxious feelings and instead make peace with them?

Then my anxiety will magically melt away all by itself?

Really?

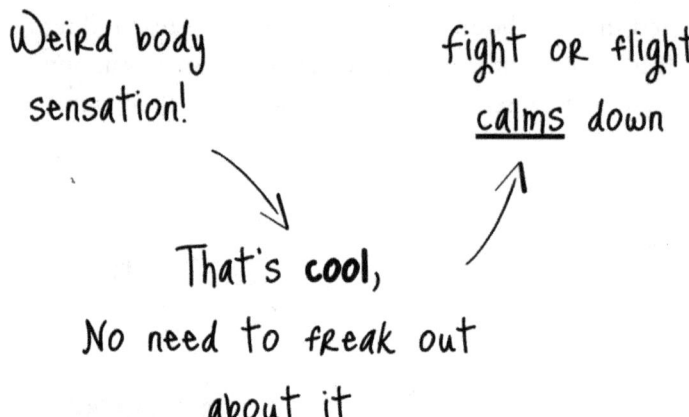

I think about it some more. For the past ten years, I've been actively resisting and fighting my anxiety — and where did that get me?

As I look over the battlefield of my life, I'm shocked by the destruction. The collateral damage is pretty extensive. Each fight with anxiety has left me a little bit more scared, worn-down, weary, isolated, fearful, judgmental and distrustful.

The war effort requires constantly lying to those who love me, keeping people at a distance, numbing my feelings and distracting my thoughts.

After ten years of fighting anxiety, the only real results are increased feelings of anger, despair and hopelessness, loss of any confidence and self-respect, and a clawing, desperate need for approval from others.

And the worst thing is that I'm no closer to being free. It's precisely because my emotional reaction to my anxiety is so intense that I keep triggering my fight-or-flight response.

Each time I try to shut out my fear, I end up strengthening it. Each time I deny its existence, I make it stronger. Each time I try to hide from it, it grows.

All of my efforts to stop it from happening are the very thing that prevents me from achieving it! Like being stuck in quicksand, the harder I struggle to break free, the more stuck I become.

For the first time ever, it all makes sense in my head.

The more I resist, the more my anxiety persists — and the more I suffer. Trying not to be anxious has been making me anxious. Trying not to have panic attacks has been ultimately causing them. In basic terms, we can put it into a simple formula:

Suffering = Discomfort × Resistance

I see myself in a never-ending tug of war, with me pulling both sides of the rope, tearing myself apart in the process. I see myself on both sides of the battlefield, attacking myself over and over again.

Fighting my anxiety has been utterly ineffective. It has all been an idiotic waste of time, effort, focus and energy. I might as well have tried to bury the ocean.

Becoming more sensitive

The worst part is that each time I failed to overcome my anxiety, I would further convince myself that I was weak, helpless and powerless against it. Each setback further strengthened the belief that I was trapped and doomed to suffer for the rest of my life.

The more scared, powerless and helpless I became, the more threatened I felt — and the more threatened I felt, the more easily I triggered my own fight-or-flight response.

As the years passed, I had become more and more sensitised to anxiety.

I had conditioned my own mind to believe that these feelings were a serious, genuine threat.

fighting anxiety TRAP

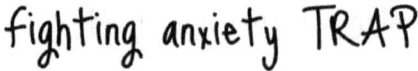

Unaware ~~fighting~~ my anxiety makes it **STRONGER!**

feel more powerless, weak and trapped

More afraid so fight back more

Yet the moment I chose to just let my anxiety do its own thing, the moment I stopped fighting, it started to melt away all by itself.

The strangest thing was that I didn't even realize I was doing it. I thought I was helping! I was just trying to avoid pain, stay safe and achieve some form of happiness.

Right then and there, I made a simple decision.

I chose to stop fighting my anxiety.

I chose to end the war and let go of resistance.

I'm on your side now, anxiety.

I declare peace.

How exactly was I going to do that I wasn't sure, but the intention was there. Maybe it would work, maybe it wouldn't. But at that moment, it didn't seem to matter. For the first time in a long time, there was a new option on the table. That in itself gave me a sense of hope.

> **Key insights:**
>
> A lifetime of rejecting fear and anxiety has conditioned us to

believe that resisting keeps us safe. It doesn't. It just keeps us trapped in an anxious state.

By having a strong emotional reaction (fear, anger, hatred, resistance) to our fight-or-flight response, we prolong and amplify it. If we stop having a strong emotional reaction and instead become more accepting and comfortable with how our fight-or-flight response makes us feel, these feelings will weaken and dissipate over time. Feel it, but don't fight it.

FIRST TRY

———

I'm on your side now, anxiety. No more fighting, no more resisting. Just me and you, in a state of glorious, blissful peace…

I step away from the computer, lie flat on the floor once again and stare up at the wood panel ceiling. Yes, I know, it's a little strange, but it helps me feel grounded, it helps me think and it helps me see things from a new perspective. Besides, there's no one around to judge.

Am I really going to allow myself to feel all my feelings and be completely okay with that?

I guess so.

Here we go. As best I can, I relax my body and open myself up to my anxious feelings. I soften into these sensations, release my control and let go of resistance.

It instantly makes me feel exposed, open and raw. I'm not used to allowing myself to feel whatever it is that I actually feel. It seems simultaneously unsettling, scary, embarrassing and wrong. It's not pleasant. If I can think of one word to describe my experience, it would be *"vulnerable"*. My confidence starts to drop rapidly.

Is this right?

Am I doing this right?

It doesn't feel right!

Am I supposed to feel this way?

Is this feeling normal?

Do regular people ever feel this way?

I'm full of doubt. I'm not sure how I'm supposed to feel. Ten years of anxiety have stripped me of the ability to feel discomfort with any sort of confidence.

I forcefully resist my knee-jerk reaction to run. I'm worried that if I don't fight this feeling, it will stay here forever. My nerves want to jump out of my skin. My legs are twitchy. I'm struggling. After a few minutes, I feel another intense wave wash over me.

WHY ISN'T THIS WORKING?!

I quickly scan my body and notice that everything in it is contracted. My jaw is clenched, my stomach is tight, my shoulders are hunched. I'm the least open and relaxed person on the planet.

Who am I trying to kid? I still have my guard up.

I'm only half-opening up — in a miserly, minimal sort of way. By opening up to my anxious feelings, I expect them to go away immediately. It's a sort of pretend acceptance, performed in the hope that doing this would cause them to quickly leave and never come back. Underneath that surface layer of acceptance is still a profound rejection and a simmering hatred towards my anxious feelings. I'm welcoming my anxiety at the front door, while hiding a loaded shotgun behind my back.

For this to work, I must stop resisting anxiety — otherwise I'll never stop triggering my fight-or-flight response. I need to let my anxious feelings intensify, I need to let them wax and wane, and all of it needs to be fine by me. It needs to be *really* fine, not just the pretend, surface-layer fine. I have to genuinely come to a place of acceptance, or I'll always be a slave to anxiety.

"Stop dipping your toes in the water, Richard, and just jump in with both feet. Let go of resistance and relax. Stop fighting!"

But I can't. My knee-jerk reaction to freak out, tense up and run is too strong.

Perhaps it's too late for me. Perhaps my behaviors are just too ingrained. Perhaps I've built up too much inner resentment, hatred and fear. For ten years, anxiety has been my torturer, my punisher and my arch nemesis. It has mercilessly destroyed my confidence, my self-esteem, my happiness, my relationships and my ability to function as a normal human being. It has traumatized me in ways I didn't even know were possible. That's why I despise it with every molecule of my being.

And now, at the flick of a switch, I'm supposed to just forget about all of that and be cool with it?

Hey, anxiety, let's hang out and be best friends! I really wish I could do that. I *really* do. But, I guess, deep down, I'm just too afraid of the feelings that anxiety inevitably stirs up.

There it is. The simple, honest truth of it all. I'm too afraid. It always comes back to fear — that most primal and powerful of emotions. Deep down, I'm simply afraid. I'm too afraid to allow myself to feel anxious. I'm too afraid to surrender and let go.

Key insights:

Making peace with anxiety is challenging. Our habitual knee-jerk reaction to resist can be strong. We need to go a little deeper in order to break free.

FU*K IT!

———

Fu*k it. If not here, then where? If not now, then when? I clean up my lunch mess and lie flat on the floor for the third time that day.

Let's run through this one last time and see if I can figure it out.

Why isn't this working? Why do I find it so challenging to make peace with my anxious feelings? Yet this morning, lying on the floor after the business meeting, I felt a sense of ease. It was almost pleasant. Why did it seem to work then and not now? What was different then?

I suppose my mindset was different. I wasn't really thinking about my anxiety. I was too busy basking in the glory of my success. I was just happy to let anxiety do its own thing. I wasn't trying to control it in any way, I wasn't expecting a certain outcome or result, and I wasn't taking it seriously.

I wasn't taking it seriously...

A 'pretend' fear

When I was around 6 years old, I became convinced that there was a monster living under my bed. I think it must have been around the time I first watched *Poltergeist* (thanks, Dad).

I'd be lying in bed and imagining this big, dark, brooding beast with sharp teeth and deadly claws crouched under my bed, just waiting to eat me up.

A part of me knew that it probably wasn't real, but I was always too scared to look under my bed to find out for sure. So, night after night, I remained fearful. Sometimes I'd fall asleep eventually. On other nights, I'd make up an excuse to sleep in my parents' bed.

After some time though, I knew that something had to change. I was a big boy of 6. I was too mature to be sleeping in my parents' bed. That wouldn't do.

So one night, I just thought, *"Darn it!"* and plucked up the courage to look under my bed. Sure enough, there was no monster there.

It was just my imagination. The monster wasn't real. It was a *'pretend'* fear that my imagination conjured up. **It was all just make-believe.**

For the next few nights, I'd look under my bed to make sure that no monsters had sneaked under it during the day. Each night, I assured myself that my fear was still just 'pretend'. Eventually, after a week or two, I was convinced that the threat wasn't real — so I stopped checking.

Every now and again, my mind would still try to conjure up monsters, but it was too late. I knew those thoughts were just my imagination, so they didn't mean anything anymore. **I didn't have to take them seriously.** I could just brush them off and let them be.

As long as I didn't give my monster thoughts much concern, my mind would eventually move on to something else. In a few months, I had forgotten all about the pretend monsters.

Anxiety is just another monster under my bed. **It's just another form of 'pretend' fear.**

The sensation of fear comes from such a deep part of my core being that it convinces me that it must be true — *but it's not*. It's just a very intense feeling of fear that actually **holds no real threat**. This feeling convinces me that I'm in danger, but in reality, **there's no danger.**

How many times have I been anxious by now? Hundreds? Thousands? And how many of them have I survived? Every… single… one.

At the end of the day, I'm not having a heart attack, I'm not suffocating and I'm not going to die or go crazy. Anxiety is just fight-or-flight chemicals rushing through my body. The jelly legs, the pounding heart, the lightheadedness are mostly just side effects of adrenaline and other stress hormones rushing through my body. The physical symptoms of anxiety are, in fact, pretty harmless. What I'm really afraid of is my own nervous system and my body's biochemical responses — which, ironically, have been **designed to keep me safe**, rather than kill me!

Just because I don't feel safe doesn't mean that I'm actually unsafe. Feeling unsafe and being unsafe are two very different things. No matter how hard my anxiety tries to convince me otherwise, **I *am* safe**.

"*Enough,*" I think to myself.

This has gone on for far too long.

I'm done playing the victim.

I'm done with anxiety bossing me around.

I'm done with this never-ending game of cat-and-mouse.

I'm calling you on your bullsh*t.

You're not real, fear.

You're just a 'pretend' fear.

I don't need to take you seriously.

I've wasted far too many years of my life running from make-believe monsters!

I think...

I exhale tension, physically soften my body, feel my mind relax, open the floodgates and let my anxiety run its course.

I feel a surge of fight-or-flight hormones in my body. Pulsing, vibrating, buzzing. My stomach drops and my skin goes clammy.

I'm not bothered.

It's just a 'pretend' fear.

It's like that overly sensitive smoke alarm that goes off whenever you cook dinner — inconvenient, loud and annoying, but **there's no real threat**.

Again I think, "*Fu*k it!*" and drop my concerns.

I like the phrase "Fu*k it!". It sums up a powerful stance and a clear intention. It's about throwing caution out the window and jumping in with both feet. It's about dismissing 'pretend' fears, being bold and taking a big step forward. It's about finally looking under the bed to see for yourself that the monsters aren't real.

Out of habit, my mind starts to worry.

"Oh, no… I don't like this. This feels wrong. I shouldn't feel like that…"

This time, however, I don't try to argue with it. I don't try to rationalize or alleviate my concerns. I don't try to outsmart my feelings or change the narrative, and I certainly don't get out my bullet point slideshow to explain to myself why I shouldn't feel this way.

I know these thoughts are just habitual worries. There's no weight behind them. I can't stop these thoughts and I'm not going to try to either. That would be a waste of my time, energy and focus. That would be me focusing on what I don't want — and that doesn't work. By putting our energy into whatever it is that we don't want, we enable it to stay.

The bottom line is that I'm safe and I have nothing to worry about. Maybe in time, as my mind gets more used to this experience, it will calm down, but for now, I don't have to give these thoughts much attention. I can simply shrug them off and pay them no heed.

"But! But! But! But!"

But… "Fu*k it!"

I don't have to listen to it or do anything to change this situation. Doing something would mean that I'm taking these concerns seriously. Doing something legitimizes the threat and proves that it *is* worthy of being cared about. But it isn't worthy. This fear is *nothing*, so it makes sense for me to *do nothing* about it.

Key insights:

Anxiety is a 'pretend' fear. You are safe.

The key to accepting anxiety is to stop taking it so seriously.

You can say, "Fu*k it!" and shrug off your concerns.

RIDING THE WAVE

And there I was, finally discovering a mindset, attitude and insight that allowed me to drop my concerns and soften into my anxiety. Saying "*Fu*k it!*" was a secret key to releasing myself from the prison of resistance.

I've never really allowed myself to experience these feelings before. I always instantly reacted, rather than calmly felt. It's the difference between freaking out when the shower suddenly goes cold and staying inside to calmly explore the cold sensation. It's tapping into that deeper, less reactive you. It actually starts to become interesting.

I have so many unanswered questions. What is this thing I'm so afraid of? How does my fear actually feel in this moment, without my imagination running amok? What happens if I don't run? What's at the end of my anxiety?

I try to *feel* what my body's actually experiencing — not an abstract idea of it, not a judgement, but the actual, living, breathing experience.

I realize that although I'm feeling fearful sensations, I'm not afraid. These are two very different things. You feel fear in your body, not in your mind. I wasn't aware of that before. My body's full of anxiety-inducing hormones, but my mind remains calm and logical about the whole situation. I'm no longer caught up in my fear, so it's easier to stay present. Rather than thinking, "Oh no! I can't believe this is happening to me!", I'm coolly observing the jitters in my stomach.

Overall, my mind feels much less reactive and more in control. It's strange that giving up control makes me feel *more* in control of my anxiety.

I feel a wave of anxiety approaching. I allow it to intensify, swell and grow.

Some emotions are *bigger* than your body. Fear is one of them. When you experience intense fear, it's not just in your bones. It occupies a space outside your body. It's in the air you breathe. It wraps its arms around you.

It engulfs you in an infinite void. Maybe it's the size of the emotion that makes people so concerned. But you know what other emotion feels bigger than your body? Excitement. Hence the phrase "bursting with excitement". Excitement is a big emotion, but it doesn't cause any concerns for anybody. In fact, the bigger, the better! So I drop my concerns about the size of my feelings.

Instead, I gladly follow my fear to see where it will go. How big will it grow? What's on the other side? As the surge rises, I follow my anxiety until it reaches full realization. No resistance, no fighting. I'm a surfer, riding the wave of my own feelings.

The wave reaches its apex. Looking down from the top of the wave, I sense all of my anxiety in its entirety. I think, "*Is this it? Is this all that there is? Is this what I've been running from this whole time? This isn't so bad!*"

Once you stop imagining how bad it's going to be and actually feel it, the experience is completely different. Once you let go of the anticipation and expectation, as in, "Oh, no… This is going to be bad!", it's nowhere near as uncomfortable or scary as you think it's going to be.

what you imagine it's like

that it's really like (without imagination)

Not so bad!

It's just simple bodily sensations

When you feel sensations in your body, it's really up to your mind to **judge your response**.

Anxiety is all about bodily sensations and judgments about those sensations. The thing is, these sensations don't have to mean anything unless you want them to. If I wasn't telling myself that something was wrong, **there would be no problem**. It's the context you put it all in that makes the difference. For one person, a roller coaster can be the best fun they've ever had, while for another, it's a terrifying nightmare. At the end of the day, nothing that awful is going on. I'm just feeling the sensations of anxiety. If I wasn't consciously resisting and fighting the way I felt, it wouldn't feel so bad.

Once you drop your expectations, concerns and imagined fears, all you're left with is **just a simple sensation of discomfort**. That's all.

It's just like feeling too cold, or too hot, or having an itch you can't scratch. These feelings belong to the same category as a sneeze or the shivers. They're just bodily sensations — **something that happens and nothing to get too concerned about**.

A few minutes later, the wave subsides and the surge weakens. I've done it. I've finally ridden the wave to its very end with no resistance. I've reached the other side of the shore. And I've survived! My world didn't fall apart, I didn't crumble to pieces, my mind didn't melt into a puddle of madness. I'm completely fine. In the end, it's been a lot of fuss over nothing.

You might look big and scary, anxiety, but you're hollow on the inside. You're all bark and no bite. All pomp and no substance. You act like you're holding all the aces, but in truth, you've got a dud hand.

You won't fool me any longer, anxiety. You're not something to be feared.

Now what?

"Now what?" I think to myself. What happens next? I've experienced anxiety at its worst and it's not even that bad. How's it going to scare me now?

Then I realize. It can't scare me. It has run out of tricks.

The penny finally drops.

Anxiety needs me to react — otherwise, it's powerless. If I don't run from it, it can't chase me. If I'm not afraid of it, it can't scare me. If I don't fight it, it can't hurt me. **The less I react, the less power it holds.**

 Key insights:

Anxiety acts all big and scary, but once you allow yourself to feel it (all of it, without resisting or letting your imagination run amok), it's nowhere near as bad as you think it's going to be. It's no big deal.

Anxiety needs you to react and be afraid of it. If you're not afraid, it's powerless.

BRINGING IT HOME

———

I'm a curious child, exploring a new world.

Anxiety is a complex multitude of tingling sensations, shifting vibrations and pulsations circulating inside my body. Always morphing, moving and changing. Sometimes intense and at other times, not so much. There's no clear divide between anxiety and my other feelings. It's all just one big melting pot of sensations.

And that's when it finally hits me. **My anxiety is me.**

Well, it's a part of me. However uncomfortable, it's still a part of the experience of *being* me. I've never thought of it that way before. Anxiety is a part of me... Those anxious sensations are a part of *my* feelings. They belong to me. Even though I don't want them, they're still *my* feelings. I've created them. That means they're an integral part of my very being. **I am the creature of my own fears.**

This simple insight changes everything.

For years, I've vehemently detested my anxiety. I was always chastizing, rejecting, berating, denying, running and blocking. Now I realize how wrong I've been. Every time I tried to run from anxiety, I was running from myself. Every time I yelled at, screamed at, hated and denied anxiety, I was doing that to myself. I was doing that to my own feelings.

Imagine that your daughter is too scared to go down the big slide at the park. How would you respond? Would you fiercely criticize her?

You suck!

You're pathetic.

You're a chicken.

I hate you.

No, of course not!

Imagine that you're bringing a new dog home and it's too anxious to go in the front door. Would you viciously attack the dog for being cautious?

No, the dog would never grow to trust you.

Imagine that your best friend comes to you for support because they're suffering from anxiety. How would you act towards them? Would you berate them, rebuke them, judge them harshly?

No, they would never be your friend again.

So why is it okay to treat yourself that way?

It's not okay. It's very far from okay. It's self-abuse — plain and simple.

Treating myself this way probably explains why I'm constantly feeling so anxious. If I treated anyone else the way I treat my own feelings, I'm sure they would be anxious too!

For the past ten years, there's been no monster under my bed, but I've sure been acting like a monster when it came to my own feelings.

By saying "Fu*k it!" and dropping the struggle, I've stopped resisting my anxious feelings. Now I take it to the next level.

I step towards my anxiety and warmly embrace it.

I welcome every one of my sensations.

Hi, jittery legs.

Hi, body flushes.

Hi, turning stomach.

I'm sorry I was so cruel to you. I realize that now, and I am so sorry. You make me feel uncomfortable, you know that? That's okay, everyone feels uncomfortable at times. I was afraid of you for so long, but now I realize how wrong that was. By hating you, I'm hating myself. By denying you, I'm denying my full capacity to live. To reject my uncomfortable feelings is to reject myself. Come here. Come back home to me. It's warm, cozy and safe. Stay as long as you wish.

I'm aware I have ten years of rejection to make up for. I can't do this half-assed. I live in Scotland, where people are known to be some of the friendliest in the world. Thirty minutes in a local pub and chances are a big, burly stranger will be giving you a bear hug. They even have a saying for it: the Scots are often referred to as being *ferociously* welcoming. I decide to cultivate a similar attitude towards my uncomfortable feelings. I *ferociously* welcome them.

I imagine a sanctuary in my mind. I make it huge. It's a special place, built expressly for my uncomfortable feelings. I give them all the room in the world to do their thing.

Slowly, my inner world starts to change.

Sensations I usually feel when anxious:

Bringing it home • 89

Sensations that I start to feel:

It's not so black and white anymore.

With each passing minute, I feel more comfortable and at ease. My body starts to induce the relaxation response. My anxiety drops from an 8.5 to about a 6. Warmth and softness melt into my stomach.

My fear and anxiety begin to melt away. Little, soft waves are spreading from the center of my body until they engulf me completely. I'm at a 5 now.

I stay on the floor for a few more minutes. It feels nice to allow myself to simply be where I am rather than where I think I need to be. My breathing is deep and slow.

I think I've just experienced a paradigm shift. A paradigm shift is defined as an important change that happens when your usual way of thinking about or doing something is replaced by a new and different perspective. I'm almost in shock because of that experience. My brain is desperately trying to figure it out and make sense of it all. There's no question that I've achieved a deeper level of understanding, compassion and peace with my anxiety.

After a while, I get up and just go about my day. I notice that I feel more settled, at peace and at ease with myself since this all began. For once, I am comfortable in my own skin.

A few hours later, Ali comes home and I excitedly tell her my story. I tell her that I don't think anxiety isn't going to be a problem for me anymore.

 Key insights:

To fight anxiety is to fight yourself.

Our emotional states are our most intimate experiences. How we treat our feelings determines the quality of our relationship with ourselves. To embrace the fullness of your humanity is to embrace all of your feelings (including fear and anxiety).

By warmly embracing your anxiety, you bring tender, compassionate feelings into the mix and help your fear to diffuse faster.

DAY 2: THE FU*K FEAR TECHNIQUE

It's the next day.

I wake up, scan my body and notice that I still feel pretty anxious. What do I expect? It's only been one day. It's probably going to take at least a few days for the medication withdrawal symptoms to wear off. In the meantime, it's best if I just accept that I'm going to be pretty sensitive. The silver lining is that this is a perfect opportunity to try out my new technique.

Will I be able to replicate the same behavior or will I fall back into my old habits of rejection, revulsion and avoidance? For the past ten years, that's been my go-to response. That habit was like a mighty river flowing through my mind. Even if I managed to get the water to flow down a new path, the old riverbed would still be there. If I wasn't careful, the flow could easily revert back.

I need to figure out a simpler way to replicate what I've gone through yesterday. If I must spend two hours wallowing on the floor, going through a big, cathartic emotional release, each time I feel anxious, it's not going to be the most practical solution. I doubt that's going to work the next time I feel anxious while out shopping.

The way I see it, the events of yesterday boil down to two distinct steps:

Step 1. I stopped taking my fears and worries about my anxious feelings seriously. I said, "Fu*k it!" to my concerns, quit struggling and simply dropped my resistance.

Step 2. Recognizing that my anxious feelings are in fact a part of me, I warmly embraced them and welcomed them home.

The result: a dramatic drop in my anxiety levels and a stronger connection to the deeper, real me.

I simplify the whole approach and put the steps into a phrase that is easy to remember and that helps me nail the right attitude, mindset and approach. I think to myself, "Fu*k it, just bring it home!"

This phrase is the core of the Fu*k Fear technique. Six words that sum up the whole approach in a neat bundle: "Fu*k it, just bring it home". So let's spend some time examining these two steps in more detail. By cementing these steps in your head, you'll make the approach much more effective.

I've kept this technique nice and simple. Simple is good. In the heat of an anxious moment, you need something simple and effective. This tool is it. Don't let its simplicity fool you. Don't underestimate how powerful this technique really is. If done right, the Fu*k Fear technique allows you to quickly relax your anxious mind and diffuse any anxious feelings.

Step 1: Think, "Fu*k it!"

When we experience a powerful anxious sensation, it can feel like it's coming from deep inside our core. It feels really personal, like it's a part of who we are. It can feel like a response to some unmet emotional need, past trauma or pain. **Even though it feels personal, we don't need to take it so personally.**

Just because you suffer from anxiety, it doesn't mean that there's something wrong with you. It doesn't mean that you're weak, broken or faulty. It doesn't mean that you haven't got what it takes or that you don't deserve to be loved. These feelings are not a reflection of who you are. They're not your soul, your innate kindness, your goodness.

All it means is that you've got a sensitive anxiety trigger. So what? Some people are sensitive to gluten. Others have skin that's sensitive to the sun. What feels good to some might feel completely overwhelming to others. You're simply less resilient to stress than other people. That's all. That's all it ever was. There's no need to take it personally.

At the same time, know that you're completely safe and these anxious feelings can't harm or hurt you in any way.

Instead, just say, "Fu*k it!" and drop your concern.

I understand that "Fu*k it!" is a very bold and somewhat provocative statement, but that's exactly why it's so effective. It's got a strong momentum and energy behind it that really helps you overcome your resistance and simply let go. It helps to snap you out of the anxiety brain fog. Sometimes "Gosh darn!' or "Flibbersticks!" just doesn't cut the mustard.

If you don't like the phrase "Fu*k it!", you can say, "Screw it!", "Bring it on!" or "Flick it!". You should play around and see what works for you. In any case, choose something that is strong, direct and acts as a clear statement of intention and attitude.

Once you've got your statement in place, you then need to *let go*. We all have an amazing ability to let go, and all you need to do is tap into that.

Have you ever played a team trust building exercise where you have to stand on the edge of a raised platform, fall backwards and rely on your teammates to catch you?

If you've tried it, you know how hard it can be to trust that you're safe enough to fall back. The solution is to forget about trying to talk yourself into doing it, and instead just go ahead and do it. At some point, you need to think, "Fu*k it!" and let go.

You can do the same with anxiety.

Make a clear decision to drop the struggle and soften your resistance. This is very much an active step. You're doing something tangible and specific here.

Initially, softening yourself in this way can feel a bit dangerous. It goes against your instincts. You may feel like you're dropping your protection — but this is a good thing. By softening your body, you lose your rock-like rigidity and gain openings, so that existence can penetrate you. **You're no longer resisting.**

Your mind may start to conjure up reasons for why this is a bad idea. *"I don't like this… It doesn't feel right…"* This is the part of you that wants you to play it safe, hang back and avoid danger. Recognize that these thoughts are simply your mind's way of trying to protect you. Your mind is just being overly cautious. But just like the 'pretend' monster under the bed, you don't have to take these thoughts seriously. Don't believe everything you think

Refuse to get caught up in the drama of these thoughts and just ignore the anxious internal narrative.

With practice, this step takes no more than 5 to 10 seconds to implement. The goal of this step is not to get rid of your anxiety, but rather to drop your knee-jerk rejection and create some breathing space. You can use that space to nurture a more helpful, compassionate response. And that's exactly where Step 2 comes in.

Step 2: Just bring it home!

This is where the magic really starts.

I want you to recognize that these uncomfortable feelings that you've been rejecting are actually an integral part of you — a part of your deep, inner self that is wounded and in pain. You may have been fighting, running away from and denying this part of yourself for years. This part of you wants to be loved, wants to be safe, wants to be at peace, wants to be recognized as good, wants to not hurt. That's why it has been chasing after you. It's been desperately wanting you to finally bring it home, to finally recover this exiled part of your being.

So let's bring it home.

For step 2 of the Fu*k fear technique I want you to embrace that part of you that has always felt alone, afraid, worried and anxious.

I want you to tap into your compassionate side and feel empathy towards your anxiety. Warmly, tenderly embrace it. Your anxiety deserves a kind, caring response.

This is an active move, not a passive one. You aren't just accepting or tolerating your feelings — you're actively embracing them. This part of yourself is vulnerable, wounded and afraid. It desperately needs reassurance. So reassure it!

"Come here. Come back home to me. It's warm, cozy and safe. I've got you. It's ok. I've nothing but time to sit here and be with you. I'm going to stay here with you through this."

Tell yourself what you've always longed to hear somebody else say.

"You are an important part of me. Of who I am. I'm will always be there for you. I'll always take care of you. Know that from now on, no matter what may come, you are not alone. I've got your back, always. You can come to me anytime. You are always welcome. "

Bring home that lost part of you and let it be present within you. Put out the welcome mat for your anxiety. Create a large internal home in your mind and invite those feelings in. Give them full permission to do whatever they wish. You're the home and anxiety is your guest. Come on in, anxiety! Feel free to roam around and do your own thing. There's plenty of room. I've made this place as comfortable as I possibly could for you. Your room has a master bed, a hot tub and a TV! Take off your shoes. Warm your socks against the fireplace. Have a rest. Stay as long as you wish — but remember, you're free to leave at any time. There's no need to stay here forever.

The trick here is to get skilled at nurturing the ideal emotional state within you. The feeling we're going for is that of being warmly welcomed or hugged. If you wish, you can imagine embracing your uncomfortable, anxious feelings. It can be a strong, rough-and-tumble sort of hug, or it can be a gentle, soft and tender one. Do whatever works best for you. You don't have to hug yourself physically — we just want to replicate the feeling of a hug. Of course, if you wish, you can give yourself a physical hug. That's okay too. Wrap your arms around your body and hold yourself for a minute.

It's important to fully commit to this process. **A half-assed approach won't cut it**. The more you embrace discomfort, the faster it diffuses and the less it bothers you. So make a clear gesture to yourself that conveys feelings of warmth, care and compassion. Think of this as unconditional acceptance of your uncomfortable feelings. Think of a mother's love for her newborn child. No strings attached. No ifs, no buts, no maybes. Embrace it all. Be willing to bring it all home. No matter what. Unconditionally. For it is all you. **To accept it is to accept yourself.**

In doing so, you set your feelings free, so they can unwind in their own time.

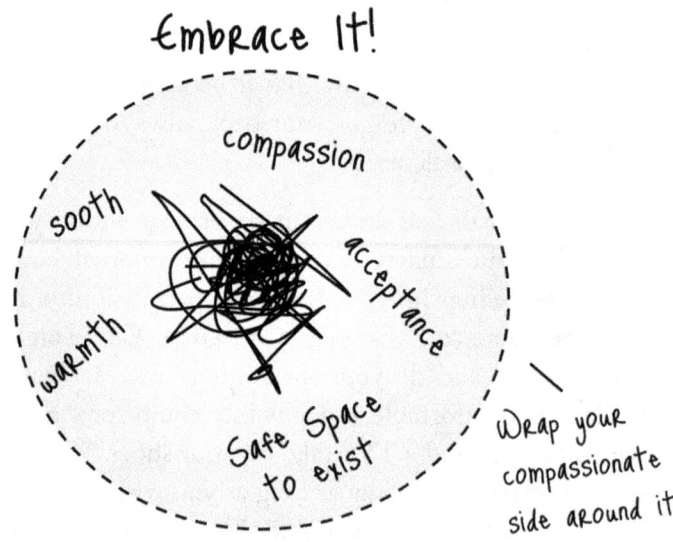

This step usually requires a few minutes of focus. Ideally, you should find a place where you can settle down and take a few minutes to generate this feeling of warmth and acceptance towards whatever you're feeling.

That's it. That's the two steps to freedom.

The Fu*k Fear technique is a skill. Like all skills, the more you practice it, the better you become at it. You need to learn how to do it. It won't grow by itself. Just like riding a bike for the first time, it may feel awkward, unnatural and a little bit funky to begin with, but it's surprising how quickly you get the hang of it.

Do it every spare moment of the day. Do it first thing in the morning. Do it whilst brushing your teeth, travelling to work, talking to someone or watching TV. As you keep on practicing it, this technique will change from something abstract and elusive to a tangible, concrete and real piece of you.

Healing with the heart

What makes the Fu*k Fear technique so powerful is that it allows you to quickly bypass your anxious brain to engage your heart. Your head thinks, "Fu*k it!", your heart embraces it.

That's important. **Healing happens in your heart.**

We all have a compassionate side to us. It's built right into our DNA. Have you ever cried at a movie? Comforted a newborn baby? Helped a friend in need? Felt sorry for the suffering of starving families all around the world? That's your compassionate side. It's there. You care about your fellow human beings, whether you recognize it or not. And if you care about others, you're more than capable of caring about yourself too.

To be honest, embracing my feelings didn't come naturally to me at all. I was raised as a Catholic in Ireland. If anything, the culture of my youth revolved around self-criticism and putting yourself down. It's a shame, really. As children, we're taught that emotions — especially nurturing, compassionate ones — are a sign of weakness or self-indulgence.

Unfortunately, being male can make recognizing that side of us even more challenging. It's manly to fight back! Real men don't cry! Men are always strong and in control! What a load of bullsh*t! All that line of thinking has done is create a generation of men who are absolutely clueless when it comes to processing any feelings of discomfort.

If there's anything I've learned over the years, it's that our compassionate side isn't a weakness — on the contrary, it might be our greatest strength.

If used right, compassion is like a superpower. If applied to our own selves, it can be far greater and far more powerful than our fear.

The opposite of fear is not courage. The opposite of fear is compassion. You cannot chase fear out. You can only bring love in. Bring compassion in, and the fear starts to subside.

Forget all about self-compassion being cowardly or soppy. Being compassionate is actually very brave because it involves taking an honest look at your own self. In order to feel compassion towards yourself, you must be willing to face your pain instead of burying your head in the sand. **That's the essence of bravery.**

Here are three reasons why this compassion-based approach is so effective:

1. Any difficult situation can be instantly improved by adding some warmth and self-compassion into the mix.

By warmly embracing our suffering and pain, we create new, positive emotions that didn't exist before. By wrapping anxiety and fear in a bundle of kindness, warmth, care, love, softness and support, we can evoke these emotions inside ourselves and alleviate our anxiety. We can create a peaceful, nurturing space within ourselves and keep our feelings and emotions safe there. Like pouring cool water on a burning fire, being compassionate towards our feelings soothes our discomfort. When our emotions feel safe, our threat detection system deactivates and our anxiety starts to melt.

2. The process of learning how to be compassionate towards ourselves teaches us that our feelings are important and deserve to be cared for. If we treat our feelings with love, we're treating ourselves with love as well. This sends a clear message to our anxious brain that we're worthy of love. We matter. We don't need to rely so much on external sources to feel good about ourselves. We can rely on our own self-compassion.

3. Self-compassion teaches us how to come to our own rescue. The unknown and the difficult is not so scary when you know how to comfort yourself. It's extremely empowering to know that we can feel loved, cared for

and watched over no matter what we're going through. It feels great to understand that we'll always be there for ourselves, no matter what life throws at us. It's a security blanket that we can take with us wherever we go, so that risks don't seem so risky. It increases our resilience to stressful or anxious situations.

Here's a little story that might help get this idea across:

A Story of Two Children

A mother has two children. One day, when they are old enough, she sends both of them off to play outside for a while and explore the world. However, the children soon run into trouble and come back a little later, feeling worried and scared.

The mother curses at her first child and scolds him for being too weak, too fearful and too soft. "It's dangerous out there! The world isn't safe enough for you! What's so good out there anyway? Why don't you just stay home from now on?"

The child loses his confidence, decides to forego the adventurous part of himself and stays at his mother's side. He refuses to go outside and play. He becomes vigilant, anxious and insecure. The boy sacrifices his freedom in order to feel safe.

When it comes to her second child, the mother decides to show compassion. She urges the child to sit beside her, hugs the child tightly and says, "Hey, kiddo, it's okay! I'll always be here to love and support you whenever you need it. It's a big world out there and it's full of adventures. You can go out, explore it and know that you'll always have a safe home to come back to. I've got your back, okay? Always." After a short rest, the child feels ready to go back outside and continue playing.

We all have that scared little child inside of us. The question is, how do you treat that child? Do you scold him? Or do you show him love and support? If you're reading this book, chances are it's the former.

Just imagine how much less intimidating and scary the world would be if you were always ready to comfort and care for yourself, whatever the circumstances! In doing so, you can play two roles at once: that of the supportive parent and of the child who's still learning to ride a bike. You're both the comforter and the comforted.

The Science

Don't just take my word for it. This is all backed up by science. Multiple studies[1] have shown that self-compassionate people tend to be much less anxious and depressed. The connection is strong here. There's no doubt about it. Self-compassion is thought to account for a massive 30 to 50% variation in how anxious or depressed people are.

A 30 to 50% variation! Let's just take a moment and allow that to sink in. By practicing self-compassion and warmly embracing your feelings, you can reduce your anxiety by half!

In other studies, self-compassion has been shown to:

• Deactivate the threat detection system and activate the self-soothing system associated with feelings of security, attachment and safety (Gilbert and Irons (2005).

• Lower the levels of cortisol, the stress hormone (Rockcliff, Gilbert, McEwan, Lightman, and Glover 2008).

• Increase heart rate variability, which is associated with a greater ability to self-soothe when stressed (Porges, 2007).

This is all due to the release of a hormone called oxytocin. By soothing your anxiety in this way, you trigger the release of this hormone (that's why it's sometimes called the cuddle hormone). The more oxytocin there is in your system, the stronger the feelings of peace, safety and connectedness are. This can result in an instant drop in your anxiety levels. Generally, you feel this as a soft, pleasant sensation of relaxation and warmth spreading out from your stomach and helping your muscles loosen up a little.

Key insights

Instead of fighting anxiety, you can:

1. Say, "Fu*k it!" and drop your concerns by not taking your fears and anxious feelings so seriously.

2. Warmly *embrace* your anxious feelings with a heart felt sense of compassion. Bring them home to you.

This will help you to disengage your anxious mind and engage your healing heart.

It can be summed up in the phrase "Fu*k it, just bring it home!"

Heads up! If you need some extra support, I've created a helpful Fu*k Fear SOS audio for you. It helps you apply the core ideas and techniques in this book when you need them most. You can download it from my website at https://ffear.co.

DAY 3: USE YOUR FOCUS

I have another business meeting scheduled for today. Typical… The reason I've started a web design business in the first place is so I can hide safely behind my computer screen all day — but, as usual, the moment I have to be highly functional, anxiety pops its head out. *"HELLO! Oh, is this a bad time? I didn't realize!"*

Thankfully, this meeting is with a long-term client, so there's less pressure to perform. All the same, I still feel on edge.

Okay, let's see how the Fu*k Fear technique works in real life.

I think, "Fu*k it! Just bring it home." I let go of my resistance, soften my body and bring my discomfort home.

I imagine my feelings and body being engulfed in a warm, white cloud of comfort, safety and homeliness. I allow myself to surrender and melt into that cloud. I allow my little cloud of compassion to form a little security barrier between me and the world. I let my feelings and thoughts feel protected, soothed and nurtured. Everything feels just a little less harsh and a little bit softer.

During the business meeting, I experience something remarkable. I'm able to focus, think clearly and communicate just fine. I am no longer a deer in the headlights.

Fighting, resisting and distracting myself from anxiety required so much mental effort from me that I could barely think straight. Now that I've finally let go of that struggle, I've gained some additional mental bandwidth and headspace.

So, how much space is there in my head exactly?

I don't know. It's difficult to give an exact figure, but I'd guess I'm operating at a capacity of about 70% at the moment.

That's great. I can hang out in that 70%. I can function there. I'm able to put my anxiety on the back shelf, letting it run amok within the remaining 30%. One part anxious, one part reasonably calm. This is wonderful. This is progress. This is much better than 100% freaking out.

Of course, I can still feel my anxiety dancing in the background. So what if it's there? I don't care. My anxiety can do the tango for all I care. I know it's just a false alarm. I continue to comfort my anxious feelings with the help of my compassion cloud. It makes me feel grounded.

As long as I allow my anxiety to do whatever it wishes, I'm able to place my focus elsewhere. I can move on with my life.

When I get home, I continue to let my anxiety take a backseat. I put my focus towards Ali. I cook us a nice meal, set the table and listen to her talk about her day. It's pleasant and calm. My fear isn't real, but the people around me are. They're much more deserving of my care, attention and focus.

Later, I'm able to lie down on the sofa and read a book. As long as I continue to embrace my anxious feelings and give them free reign to do whatever they want, I can focus on other things.

Focus on life

Most of us don't know this, but our ability to focus is one of our greatest strengths. Studies show that we have little to no control over our emotions, feelings or thoughts — however, one of the very few things that we can control is our focus. That's what makes it so useful.

Have you ever had a conversation with your friend in the middle of a noisy restaurant? There are people talking, plates clanging, silverware clattering… Yet you're able to drown out the noise and just listen to your friend. That's focus.

After applying the Fu*k Fear technique and accepting our emotions, we can move our focus elsewhere.

Instead of focusing on our anxious feelings, we can choose to **place our attention on the life that's unfolding around us**. We can allow ourselves to get absorbed in hobbies, interests, conversations, work, nature, whilst allowing our anxiety to run amok in the background.

The point is, by no longer putting all of our energy into fighting what we don't want (anxiety), we can redirect our energy towards the things we do want (life!).

I must stress, however, that changing the object of your focus is very different from distraction. Distraction requires a huge mental effort because you're trying to block out your anxiety and fear completely. Ironically, the mental effort required to block out anxiety eats up all of your attention and focus. Blocking anything out just doesn't work.

As a little tip, sometimes, if I'm stuck for something to focus on other than fear and anxiety, I focus on my toes. It sounds silly, but your toes are never stressed (well, at least mine aren't). It can also be helpful to feel your feet placed firmly on the floor. You can tune into the sounds around you, the seat beneath you, the sky or ceiling above you — whatever is happening in the present moment. The more connected you feel to the world around you, the more grounded you'll feel.

> **Key insights:**
>
> Focus is extremely powerful. After applying the Fu*k Fear technique, place your focus elsewhere. Redirect your energy towards the things you enjoy and just let your anxiety do whatever it wants in the background. It's just a 'pretend' fear. You're not bothered by it.

DAY 4: EMBRACE DUALITY

There's no doubt in my mind that this approach is working. With each passing day, I feel another layer of anxiety peel off and fall away. As I become more experienced at the Fu*k Fear technique, it starts working quicker and is more effective. My confidence is steadily growing — yet at the same time, I observe that something odd is going on.

I get that by bringing my discomfort home, I'm adding new feelings of warmth and compassion into the mix, which is great, — but the feeling of **discomfort still remains.** *I'm still anxious.* Perhaps the edges of my anxiety get a little softer, but it's still there nonetheless.

Now there are two *opposing* parts of me: a part of me feels warmth, love and acceptance, yet a different part experiences discomfort and dread. A part of me wants to embrace my anxious feelings, and a part of me wants to reject them. A part of me wants to run, and a part of me wants to stay. A part of me hates how I feel, and a part of me is okay with all of my feelings.

It's a delicate balance. I'm worried that a light breeze is going to bring the whole thing crashing down like a house of cards.

How can two opposite feelings exist within the same space? It's confusing. It doesn't make sense. Am I doing this wrong? Why is there a part of me that is still resisting?

This is probably a good time to introduce to you the concept of duality.

Letting go of the black-or-white

We get so caught up in the idea that everything has to be this or that, one thing or the other, black or white — but the truth is a lot more nuanced and complex. We can experience things that are both good and bad, both black and white. We can feel excited to start a new project, yet the prospect can also scare us. We can crave adventure and miss the safety of our home. We can feel anger towards a family member and still know that it is undercut with a deep sense of love. We can ride a roller coaster and feel fear, yet know that we're completely safe.

We can do this due to the remarkable power of duality (well, that's what I like to call it, anyway). Duality is the ability of our mind to hold two diametrically opposed beliefs at the same time.

The idea of duality is very, very helpful if you're trying to overcome your anxiety.

I want you to let go of the idea that we're trying to get rid of anxious feelings. That's *never* going to be the case. We're not trying to replace anxious feelings with positive ones. If your anxiety subsides, that's great — but making it subside is not the goal. This is one of the most common mistakes people make when trying to get over anxiety.

The goal is to tenderly embrace our discomfort and pain, **whilst still allowing that discomfort to exist**. It's to *get comfortable with being uncomfortable.*

Even if you fully embrace and welcome your anxiety and discomfort, there may still be a part of you that would rather fear and anxiety wasn't there. There may always be a part of you that wants to constrict, run and hide. There's absolutely nothing wrong with this. That part of you is just as valid as any other part. You can allow that side of you to exist.

Opposing emotions exist inside all of us. A part of you may want to resist fear and anxiety, yet a part of you may want to accept them. You can feel safe and unsafe at the same time. You can feel unease and you can feel comfort. You can experience feelings that you like and feelings that you don't like. Duality.

Many of us don't realize it, but two opposites can happily coexist in our minds. Yes, it doesn't make perfect sense. But that's okay. Who says that your feelings have to make sense anyway? Feelings are only confusing if you try to make sense of them. There's no need to waste your time and energy trying to figure them out or resolve the conundrum.

Let go of the need to understand your conflicting feelings. These two sides don't have to fight each other. There's no need to declare one winner.

It's better to accept that some things are just the way they are. You don't need to overanalyze them. It's when you put thoughts in charge of feelings that you get into trouble. No other animal on the planet tries to make sense of its emotions — so why should we?

Just open up your mind and allow all conflicting feelings and emotions to comfortably exist side by side.

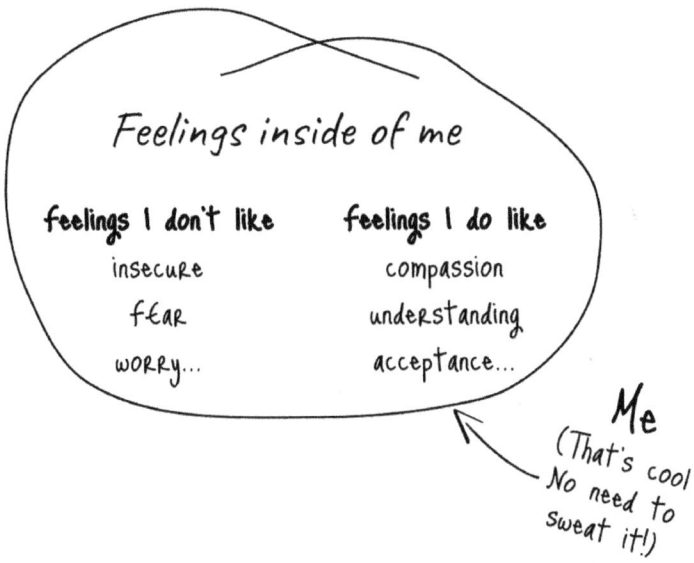

I truly believe that duality is the secret key to overcoming fear and anxiety. Not only does it remove the pressure for your emotions to make sense or fit inside a comfortable box, but it also shows that you don't have to be *unconditionally* at peace with yourself.

Recognizing my inner duality has ultimately helped me embrace my feelings fully. It's okay if one part of me wants to run and hide. That's perfectly understandable. It's okay if one part of me is frustrated and fed up — that's only natural. There's enough space within me for all of my emotions, even if they don't always agree with each other.

Keep in mind though that duality can feel a little funky to begin with. We like order and we like things to make sense. The good news is that it becomes surprisingly easy and very liberating once you get the hang of it. In time, you'll become fascinated by your ability to feel fragile, vulnerable, strong, complicated, anxious and brave all at once. We're multifaceted beings. Heads and tails may be opposites, but they're still two sides of the same coin.

Key insights:

We're not trying to replace anxious feelings with positive ones. On the contrary, you can generate positive feelings by *showing compassion* towards your anxiety and allowing it to exist. Afterwards, you may observe conflicting — both comfortable and uncomfortable — feelings within you. Allow for that duality.

If you are looking for extra guidance on the Fu*k Fear technique go to https://ffear.co and access the bonus tools and materials.

DAY 5: DROP THE FANTASY

"Oh, good morning, anxiety! You're still here, huh? Again?!"

"Really? Come on! Did we not go through this sh*t yesterday?"

The initial novelty of embracing my anxiety is wearing off. I'm not feeling so enthusiastic today.

"Okay, anxiety, can you do me a favor? Can you just give me a break — just for today? You see, I didn't sleep well last night and I've got a bunch of chores that need to be done. Can't you please just give me a day off? No?"

I'm tempted to punch my anxiety in the face. But, of course, I'd just be punching myself.

Sometimes embracing anxiety can be a real pain in the ass. Sometimes you just want to get on with your life without having to deal with this burden. Although this is the path to freedom, at times it may feel like the exact opposite.

Patience is the name of the game. When you're feeling anxious, you're desperate for the feeling to go away — but if you've triggered your fight-or-flight response earlier on, your body is now flushed with anxiety hormones, which can take hours or even days to clear out of your system. It's like waiting for boiling water to cool: it simply takes time. Our suffering is caused by the desire for things to be different than they are.

All the same, saying that I need patience is one thing, but *being* patient is entirely different. Embracing my anxiety feels like an eternity of torture. It's an itch I just can't scratch.

I want to scream to the heavens, "THIS SHOULD NOT BE HAPPENING! MY LIFE IS NOT SUPPOSED TO BE THIS WAY! I SHOULD BE ABLE TO GET RID OF MY SUFFERING!"

A part of me hates me for feeling like this. I feel as though my suffering makes me a lesser human being.

But why?

Who says that I should never feel any discomfort or pain?

Am I better or somehow more special than everyone else?

Or am I simply human, just like the rest of us — with all of my human issues, human concerns and human struggles?

For years, I've been trying to live up to the idea of the old, pre-anxiety Richard — this wonderful, fantastic version of me who is always happy, upbeat and confident. But nothing can ever match such a ridiculously high standard. I'll never be happy enough, funny enough, confident enough, special enough.

Without realizing it, I've turned into a bridezilla. A bridezilla is a woman whose behaviour in planning the details of her wedding is regarded as obsessive or intolerably demanding. Bridezillas come about because they put so much pressure on themselves for their wedding day to be perfect.

Yet the pressure to be perfect causes smaller and smaller things to bother them. Everything is judged harshly against their impossibly high standards. The napkins are the wrong colour! The curtains don't match! They terrorize their bridal party, make ridiculous demands and stress everyone out. What should be one of the happiest days of their lives can easily turn into misery, simply because it is *never* perfect enough.

For the past ten years, I've been a bridezilla to my own feelings. The more I've tried to live up to the dream of the old, pre-anxiety Richard, the harsher I've judged my feelings and the more I've suffered.

That's the difficult thing about feelings: they're unique to you and totally unavailable to the rest of the world. The only person who knows exactly how you feel is you. But that means that the only person who can judge your feelings is also you.

Somewhere along the line, I've decided to measure all of my feelings against the pre-anxiety me — and, of course, everything has come up short.

Why do I place such high standards on my own feelings?

Why am I putting so much pressure on myself?

It's not like there's an official, standardized government chart for me to measure my feelings against. We don't have the equivalent of a body mass index when it comes to emotions. I've done this to myself. I've created my own imaginary standard to flog myself against.

So I'm sensitive to anxiety. What's wrong with that?

So I feel a bit shit today. Is that such a huge problem?

In what reality can I honestly expect to feel wonderful and fantastic *all* the time and never experience a moment's discomfort?

It all boils down to this: are my problems caused by the way I feel? Or are they caused by what I'm telling myself about how I feel?

It's **my judgment of my feelings that is causing these issues**. If I didn't judge my feelings so harshly, they wouldn't be such a problem.

When will I accept that my experience with anxiety has changed me? I haven't seen the old me in more than a decade, for Christ's sake! That's not who I am right now. I'm older, wiser, more battleworn and scarred. That's my reality. Why don't I allow myself to grow and change as a person?

It's time to lower my ridiculous standards and accept the person I am now, rather than struggle endlessly to be someone else. *Au revoir*, wonderful fantasy Richard! My happiness will no longer depend on how successful I am at becoming you.

I must drop this fantasy and instead embrace my humanity and my human feelings just as they are, at this very moment. I'm all I've got. Me. Right here, right now. This is all there has ever been. I will have to do.

A part of me feels a little sad giving this fantasy up. A part of me still wishes that I could click my heels three times and go back to the way things used to be. But it turns out that life isn't like the movies. In life, you can never go back to Kansas.

Another part of me, however, feels a huge sense of relief. A weight has been lifted off my shoulders. I've finally taken off my mask. No pressure to be super confident. No pressure to be wonderfully fantastic. No pressure to be free of anxiety. No more pretending. No more hiding. No more faking.

"Hello, my name's Richard and I'm sensitive to anxiety. It's nice to finally meet you!"

I immediately feel a sense of ease as I allow myself to be imperfectly me.

Besides, my reality isn't so bad after all. I have my health, I have Ali, I have shelter, food, clothes and access to modern conveniences. I have arms that can hug my loved ones. I have a voice that allows me to talk (and sing cheesy songs, badly). I have eyes so I can see the beauty in the world. I can walk outside, smell the fresh air and see nature in all of its glory. I'm free to live my life as I choose. By all conventional metrics, life's good.

Perhaps these things are wonderfully average. Perhaps they don't seem special to others at all. However, anxiety forces us to lose touch with these things. By letting go of the fantasy and bringing my focus back to the here and now, I begin to realize just how wondrous that here and now actually is.

Besides, I guarantee that there are plenty of people out there who've had it way worse. In the grand scheme of things, a little anxiety is no excuse to lose sight of what matters in life.

True contentment is here and now

Something wonderful happens when you let go of the fantasy and embrace your humanity. You no longer waste so much time and energy trying to change. You spend less time comparing yourself to other people (or an older, less anxious version of you). You no longer feel dissatisfied with yourself or your life. It liberates you.

The Gap (resolved)

DREAM LIFE

drop the fantasy

The Gap
(Not a PROBLEM anymore)

where I WANT to be

REAL LIFE

True contentment is all about noticing the amazing life that's unfolding all around us, without any fantasies clouding our vision. The people, the experiences, the adventures, the connections, the wonders of nature… You can notice all of these things right at this moment. They're always available to you. The joy that they bring is not the climactic high that we associate with excitement or stimulation, but rather a deep sense of awe and wonder that can suffuse the most ordinary things and the most ordinary moments with quiet, all-encompassing bliss.

> **Key insights:**
>
> When we drop the fantasy, we feel less dissatisfied with life.
>
> The more we notice and appreciate the goodness in our surroundings, the happier we are.

DAY 6: BRING YOURSELF HOME

Dropping the fantasy feels good. I've grown tired of the endless struggle to be someone else. There is a lot of relief in that — but at the same time, if I'm honest, I feel miserable today.

I feel some old pains rising up from the depths of my soul. Sadness, grief and shame that have been buried inside me are bubbling to the surface. Now that I've allowed myself to feel, I'm starting to feel all of it. Warts and all. Discomfort and comfort. Darkness and light. Ugliness and beauty.

I'm tempted to push the feelings away and ignore my pain, but I've already spent too many years running from myself. If I'm to embrace the fullness of my humanity, I must embrace all of it — the positive, the negative and the neutral.

I can't pick and choose what parts of me to accept and be okay with. I can't choose to only experience happiness and joy or to never have any feelings of sadness and pain. To be fully awake to life means showing up for both the easy and the difficult, the joyous and the sorrowful.

What's the point of being here and being human if I can't embrace the human condition in its entirety?

So, as best I can, I try to embrace my feelings.

It's the weekend, so I give myself full permission to take the day off. I drag the sofa in front of the TV and spend a few hours watching cheesy sci-fi movies from the 1980s (*Star Trek 2* and *Star Trek 3* if you're curious). Afterwards, I cook myself some comfort food (creamy pasta) whilst dancing to my favourite music in the kitchen. Then, with a warm blanket and a full stomach, I curl up on the sofa again, reading *Calvin and Hobbes*. Basically, I do anything I feel like doing — 100% guilt-free.

How does it make me feel, you wonder?

It makes me feel great! For the first time ever, I acknowledge that my pain and suffering deserve a kind, caring response. It's nice to embrace the part of me that has always felt alone, abandoned and unsupported. Even amongst the discomfort, it feels good to be cared for. The experience is one of spending the day with someone who loves me unconditionally, who doesn't judge me and who doesn't think it's wrong to pamper myself a little when I'm feeling down.

In truth, that day turned out to be one of the best days I'd ever had. Now I do it all the time. I love a good *me party*.

Learning to look after yourself

That day, spent lying on the sofa, doing nothing much in particular, made me realize something crucial: **the way I treat myself when I'm suffering is more important than getting over it.**

Too often we beat ourselves up just because we're suffering. We see our suffering as evidence that we're not worthy of love. We end up treating ourselves most harshly precisely when we need to support ourselves the most.

However, to really break free from anxiety and fear, it's imperative that we learn to look after ourselves.

If you accidentally burned your hand under a hot tap, you'd immediately care for and nurture the wound. Why don't we do the same when we're feeling down?

If you're unable to be kind to the one person who needs it most (i.e. you), you'll never be able to be truly kind to others. We need to nurture our innate kindness from within. We should all cultivate that inner space. If we tend to our inner gardens first, we become much better at being kind to others.

I get it though. It can be challenging to be kind to yourself if you suffer from anxiety. But you're not alone. We all have parts of ourselves that we struggle with. We all have parts of us that feel ugly. We all have doubts, fears and insecurities. We all have days when we feel like we're not good enough, not smart enough, unworthy of love. We all have days when our confidence abandons us. We all feel extra sensitive, on edge and stressed from time to time. Welcome to the human race!

You don't have to feel 100% good about yourself in order to care for yourself — nor does anyone else. You can care for yourself despite having parts of you that you don't like. Even with all of your faults and weaknesses, you're worthy of care and love. You're human. You're alive. You are here and now. You're good at your core. These are all the reasons you need to feel love for yourself.

LOOK AFTER YOUR NEEDS

If you're feeling down right now, try not to judge this experience so harshly. Try not to be so critical of the way you feel. Feeling this way doesn't make you a failure. It makes you human. No one is immune to stress, fatigue and negative feelings. We've all been there. It's okay to have negative thoughts and feelings. Humans are a little negative by nature, so it's natural to feel down from time to time.

All feelings are a part of life. All emotions are valid and important. They enrich, color and amplify our existence. Grief helps you slow down and contemplate life. Anger helps you stand up for your beliefs. Doubt helps you assess your skills. Sadness is a healthy response to loss. Anxiety can let you know that you're currently in a difficult situation. It's okay to have feelings and emotions, both comfortable and uncomfortable. That's what being human is all about.

Instead of judging yourself, embrace your feelings and **think of something you can do to care for yourself.**

A great question I always recommend asking yourself is this: what would you tell your best friend if they were in the same situation?

This may be the single most powerful question when it comes to making personal decisions.

I know we've all heard that phrase before, but how many of us have actually done it? People really underestimate how powerful this strategy is. Don't knock it until you try it.

How would you support a friend going through the same struggles right now?

How much patience and kindness would you show them?

How would you send them love?

Think about it. And then, if possible, do the exact same thing for yourself.

Don't be afraid to go BIG! Be much kinder and more supportive to yourself than you think you should be. Your compassion muscle is probably so weak right now that it desperately needs a decent workout. Just think of how often you've practiced rejection, denial and hatred of your feelings! It's helpful to counterbalance those habits.

 Key Insight

> Bring yourself home. Rather than try to change your feelings, you can embrace them and treat yourself as you would treat a good friend.

DAY 7: EMBRACE YOUR HUMANITY

Nothing much exciting happened today. So, instead I'm going to use this opportunity to go on a little rant…

Why do we always think that our anxiety is special or unique?

It's not.

The latest research shows that almost 1 in 5 people suffer from anxiety issues[1]. Just think about that for a second. That's 20% of the population! Literally millions of people in your country are going through the same thing you are RIGHT NOW.

If anything, your anxiety, worries and fears might even be boringly commonplace!

I wish someone would invent special glasses that would allow us to see how everybody's feeling on the inside. Just for one day a year, everyone would get to see how everyone else feels. It would be amazingly cathartic. We'd realize that we all feel similar worries, anxieties, and struggle with similar stressors. We'd realize that we're not alone in our suffering and we never have been.

We're all human. Like all humans, we feel insecure, not good enough, inadequate, disappointed, sad, unloved at times. This is all part of being human. This is all part of life. The fantasy that everyone else is living a perfectly happy life is just that: a fantasy.

We get caught up in this idea that everyone is more successful and generally better than us. Social media — Facebook, Instagram and the like — is full of beautiful people enjoying their shiny, perfect lives. But the truth is that it's all fiction. It's just another fake story. It isn't real life. It's just people showing you their storefronts and hiding all of the messy stuff in the backroom. Life's hard — for everybody. We all grow old, decay and die. Fact. We all lose our loved ones. Fact. We all experience heartbreak, heartache, suffering and pain. Fact. This is the reality of life.

My point is that everybody goes through some sort of suffering in this life. Depression, eating disorders, drug addiction, being bullied at school, family issues, health issues and, of course, anxiety — you name it, somebody's definitely got it.

There are hundreds of people in your local area going through the exact same issues with anxiety. Your neighbour, your postman, the teacher of your kids might all be just as anxious as you are. Allow this fact to comfort and nourish your soul. You may or may not get a chance to discuss your struggles face to face with these people one day, but it's still the absolute and honest truth that you're not, never have been, never will be alone in this.

Embrace your common humanity. I know only too well how lonely anxiety might feel, so please, let me stress:

> You're not alone in your suffering!
> You're not alone in your suffering!
> You're not alone in your suffering!

Let go of "Why me"

Here's another little rant…

Have you ever asked yourself, "Why me? Why do I have to be the one who suffers?"

I used to do that all the time.

I want to share a story with you. A good friend of mine finally got pregnant after trying for a baby for a number of years. Sadly, there were complications during the pregnancy and the baby was born with serious health issues. Despite everyone's best efforts, the baby lived for just a few short weeks. It was an extremely tragic and sad time in their — and our — lives. We were all completely heartbroken.

A few months later, we all met up and I was amazed at how much life was still inside my friend. Sure, she was in great pain, but she was also open and engaged. She was so brilliantly alive that I could see her heart, full of love and care, shining out of her body.

I asked her how she could be so strong after such a crippling tragedy. She then told me how the question "Why me?" kept spinning around and around in her brain... until one day she flipped that question upside down.

"Why *not* me?"

Why would she wish that pain and suffering on someone else?

Why was suffering okay for others, but not for her?

She realized that it wasn't okay. So she decided to accept her suffering. She decided to own it, so that other people wouldn't have to. It was an unbelievable show of strength and acceptance during an incredibly challenging time.

If we can apply as little as one percent of that acceptance and understanding to our anxiety, we can help alleviate our suffering. We can let go of the question "Why me?" and instead ask ourselves, "Why not me?"

 Key Insights

> Everybody's got their own struggles. Remember that and go easy on yourself. Embrace your humanity and your human flaws.

DAY 8 FORGIVE YOURSELF

I'm sorry.

I'm not exactly sure why it's taken me this long to forgive myself for my anxiety. I guess I was disappointed in myself for having a perceived flaw.

I'm sorry.

Over this past week of opening up to my feelings, I've noticed I'm still holding a deep, quiet, residual anger towards myself.

I'm sorry.

I think these feelings of disappointment and anger have lain dormant in me for years. They feel ancient.

I'm sorry.

Sorry for what?.. Sorry for hating myself because I'm not perfect enough.

Sorry for being so ashamed of who I am.

Sorry for taking so long to come to my own rescue.

Sorry for having to go through all that I've gone through.

I'm so sorry.

The more I forgive myself, the more I let go of that sense of anger and blame. I'm less burdened. I feel more free.

I'm so sorry.

But it's not like flicking a light switch. I need to do it over and over to really let it sink in.

I'm so, so sorry.

It truly is strange when you think about it: if I broke my arm, everyone would be sympathetic about my struggle. However, because my anxiety is internal, no one is able to see it — so there's no sympathy from anyone. Especially not from my own self. That's a mistake I don't intend to make again.

I'm so sorry.

Tears start streaming down my face. It's okay if I'm sensitive to anxiety. It's okay to just be me. I'm good enough as I am.

If you suffer with anxiety, I recommend you forgive yourself too. There is a lot of power in forgiveness.

It's a simple choice. You can do it right now. Spend a couple of minutes alone and forgive yourself for your history with anxiety. Let go of any sense of blame. Remind yourself that it's not your fault that you're sensitive to anxiety. You're trying your best under the circumstances, and that's all you can really ask of yourself.

You can even look in the mirror and say, "I forgive you." Try to do this at least once a day to nurture a growing sense of forgiveness towards your suffering.

Key Insights

 Forgive yourself for your anxiety. It's not your fault.

DAY 9: STRUGGLING TO BRING HOME

I'm having a bad day. It's not working.

I can't drop my struggle, I can't bring my feelings home, everything just feels clumsy, awkward and forced. I try again for the tenth time this hour. I sit down, compose myself, soften my body and say, "Fu*k it! just bring it home"

After five minutes, it becomes clear that it's just not happening. I don't feel much of anything. No warmth, no ease, no kindness. I'm just not feeling very self-compassionate today.

Nevertheless, I refuse to give up. Rather than doing that, I stack another level of compassion on top. I bring home the fact that I'm struggling today. As best I can, I allow myself to feel compassion towards the fact that I'm struggling to feel compassionate.

Another five minutes go by and I realize that this too isn't getting me anywhere. I'm not doing a great job of being compassionate towards my own lack of self-compassion.

That's okay. I can stack another level of acceptance on top of the previous one.

So I bring home the fact that I'm struggling to bring home the fact that I'm struggling to bring home my anxious feelings. Yes, I know it sounds a bit ridiculous, but I finally notice that it does help a little. I'm not feeling wonderful by any stretch, but it takes the edge off. We all have bad days. Today is my bad day and right now, I feel a little more okay, a little more compassionate towards that fact.

Level up compassion

"Fu*k it. Just bring it home!" is a power move. It trumps everything. Just like stacking a Russian doll, you can always go one level higher. Everything can be embraced within the warm, caring support of compassion — even the fact that you're not feeling very compassionate!

THIS SUCKS!
↓ feel compassionate towards my struggle

THIS STILL SUCKS!
↓ feel MORE compassion towards struggle

STILL SUCKY!
↓ and... MORE compassion

Sucky! + some compassion

Ok, that feels a little better. Thanks.

Here are some other strategies you can use when you're struggling to bring anxiety home.

Visualization

Sometimes I would visualize my anxiety as my older brother — except that in my mind, he was eight years old and throwing mud balls at me.

Let me explain. I love my brother dearly. He's easily one of my favorite people on Earth. However, when we were kids, torturing me was his favorite pastime. He was always picking on me, poking me, bullying me. I used to dream of the day when I'd grow up to be big and strong, so I could finally kick his ass. Of course, by the time I grew up, all had been forgiven and we had become the best of friends.

Did I hate him at times? Certainly. He was the bane of my otherwise happy six-year-old existence.

Did I struggle to accept and embrace him? You bet.

But did I ever want to get rid of him? Absolutely never.

Did I love him? Completely, without hesitation.

The image of my brother was perfect when it came to capturing both my struggle with anxiety and the compassion that I had started to feel towards it.

In my imagination, my brother was wearing red shorts and a striped T-shirt. For some inexplicable reason, he was throwing mud balls at me. He looked ridiculous. He was knee-deep in mud, covered in it — and his aim was way off. I'd imagine him trying to bully me again, but his attempts were rather pathetic.

I recognized deep inside me that although he was trying to bully me, I still genuinely and warmly loved him. My love and compassion for my brother ultimately outweighed any frustration, fear or hatred that I might have felt towards him. My love trumped my fear. Compassion won. Ridiculous? Yes. A bit strange? Sure! But in my head, it made perfect sense. A simple image that allowed me to feel compassion towards something that I was struggling with. A neat visualization that made it much easier for me to embrace anxiety, even when I was feeling particularly fed up and frustrated with it.

Create your own visualization

If you wish to create a visualization of your anxiety, here are three helpful tips:

1. You must deeply love it.

Start by thinking of something that makes it easy for you to get your compassion juice flowing. Whatever you visualize, it's very important to feel a strong sense of love towards it. Family members work well here: your brother, sister, mom, dad, your children, nieces or nephews, your first love, even the family dog or cat! Close friends are okay too — or you can even visualize yourself as a child.

2. Imagine it being annoying right now.

Let's be honest: anxiety is a pain in the ass. It's annoying and we'd rather not deal with it. So let your visualization reflect the annoying aspect of your anxiety. This part is important, as it recognizes the duality of our feelings. Loving something, but at the same time being frustrated with it. Wanting to accept it and at the same time, wanting to reject it completely.

Perhaps it's your brother or sister bullying you as a kid. Perhaps it's you as a child, wailing at your parents. No matter how annoying your mental image is, the key condition here is that your love must ultimately outweigh any negative emotions that you feel towards it.

3. Make it silly.

Silly works brilliantly here. Silly is your friend. We tend to imagine fear as very serious, dark, brooding and dangerous, but our minds are fully capable of painting a very different picture. Nothing undercuts the seriousness as well as a bit of playfulness and silliness does. So make your mental image a bit ridiculous.

Perhaps your dog is only two inches tall. It's trying to look scary, but, in all honesty, it's about as threatening as a daisy. You can throw a funny hat on its head, make the colors bright or have bubbles coming out of its ears — just set your imagination free!

Ultimately, though, when you look at this mental image, you want to feel love. A deep, tender, unconditional love. This will make bringing your feelings home much easier. When you catch yourself experiencing anxiety or fear, associate this image with them immediately. It won't take long for it to become a habit.

Make it silly

Affirmations

Affirmations can be extremely helpful too. They serve to clarify, refocus and bolster your intended emotional state.

Here are some examples of affirmations — or mantras — you can use during the process of befriending your anxious feelings:

"I am safe, I am loved, I am held."

"No matter what, I'm here for all of me."

"Hey buddy, I've missed you! Come on in for a snuggle!"

"I'm having a really hard time right now, but that's okay. I'm human."

"May I be gentle and understanding towards myself."

Of course, as always, you should play around and discover what works best for you. If the mantra that works for you turns out to be something like "*Gooooooo, heart power!*", that's absolutely fine. Being playful and silly helps to diffuse the 'seriousness' of fear and anxiety.

Play around with it

Everybody is different. Everybody's life, history and journey is different. Everybody's experience of fear and anxiety is different. This isn't a one-size-fits-all technique. Feel free to play around, adapt and adjust things to suit your individual needs. Think of it as a Fu*k Fear buffet. You can pick and choose the bits you like best, mix them up in any way you wish and ignore the bits you don't want. There are no rules. What works best for you *is* best for you.

 Key insight:

> Be creative with the Fu*k Fear technique. Discover what works best for you. You can try levelling up your compassion, visualizing your anxiety or repeating affirmations.

DAY 10: BRINGING THE CATASTROPHE HOME

I'm caught in a nasty traffic jam. I'm going to be late for a meeting with an important client. I feel myself getting upset, agitated and angry. Inside, I'm screaming, "MOVE IT!!!" at the car in front of me, but, unsurprisingly, it's not working. The car stubbornly refuses to "move it". My stress levels are rapidly rising.

I'm aware that I'm resisting reality again. I'm trying to force situations to be the way I want them to be. I'm creating my own tension.

Really, this isn't about the traffic jam. It's about control.

How many things do we have control over in our life?

Just about zero, right?

But that doesn't stop us from *trying* to control everything. And this is a major source of tension and stress.

Every day we try to hustle and get by as best we can, juggling 20 different balls at once. We've got work commitments, bills to pay, relationships to attend to, emotional issues to deal with, health to maintain, chores to do, responsibilities to fulfil, on and on and on.

And as soon as we feel we've got a handle on things, something else pops up. Some unexpected, new issue lands in our lap and we have to deal with that shit too.

Modern life is a catastrophe. It's a series of crises, disasters and little things that go wrong along the way. And, to top it all off, we all grow old, get sick and die eventually.

Trying to resist or fight against that tidal wave of fu*kedness is pointless.

We can't control it. The only thing we *can* control is our response.

"The truth is that stress doesn't come from your boss, your kids, your spouse, traffic jams, health challenges, or other circumstances. It comes from your thoughts about these circumstances." — Andrew J. Bernstein

So here's the deal. Things won't always go your way in life. Stuff happens. Stress will alight on your shoulders, just like it does on everybody else's. The question is, how do you want to deal with it?

You can resist it, fight it, get angry with it, but it won't improve the situation. The catastrophe of life will continue to unfold. And you'll waste a whole lot of energy denying something that's already a fact.

Or you can choose to think, "Fu*k it! Just bring it home!"

Instead of fighting it, open up your arms to the gale of life's experiences. Surrender control and embrace the journey.

Embracing it doesn't mean that you're satisfied with the way things are or that you're resigned to tolerating them as they "have to be". Embracing it simply means seeing things as they are. It means taking each moment as it comes and being with it fully, just as it is. That way, it doesn't weigh you down so much. You can navigate around it.

So, as best I can, I bring the catastrophe of the moment home.

Hey stress ball in my mind. Nice to meet you again. It makes sense that you are here. It's a stressful situation, but I don't need to make things worse by struggling or fighting against you.

So I'm caught in a traffic jam. So what? It's not the end of the world. I'm sure the graveyard is full of people who would like to be alive and stuck in a traffic jam. I'm just going to hang out and as best I can just let things be as they are.

And with that, I feel a sense of ease.

 Key insight:

> We have little control over how our life unfolds. When life throws something at you, rather than fighting it, it's better to just roll with it. Bring the catastrophe home.

DAY 11: STOP LOOKING FOR IT

I wake up and habitually scan my body, searching for any signs of anxiety. The coast is clear. I don't feel anxious today! Woohoo!

Wait a second… What's that strange sensation at the back of my head? Is that it?.. It could be… What if it is!

And then I catch myself. Why am I looking for it? What happened to my attitude of "Fu*k it"?! Am I not supposed to be indifferent to it? If I was truly indifferent, I wouldn't go searching for it, would I? True indifference means not caring if it's there or not.

Does this sound familiar to you? Have you ever done this? Have you gone looking for your anxiety?

I used to do that all the time. I'd wake up in the morning and, for a brief moment, my mind would bask in that comfortable state between being asleep and being awake. The morning sun would be peeking through the curtains. The air would be quiet and still. A moment of peace… And then I'd remember that I suffer from anxiety. I'd immediately go searching for it. I'd keep on searching until I convinced myself that I had found the evidence I needed.

"Well, I guess my stomach's feeling a little queasy."

It might have been just because I was hungry, but that wouldn't matter to me. I'd immediately convince myself otherwise.

"That's it. It's still here! Noooo!"

I'd feel a dreadful sense of despair and anguish crash down on me like a sledgehammer. My fight-or-flight response would kick in — and that would be it. My day was ruined. My anxiety had enslaved me once again.

The strange thing was that I'd be perfectly fine beforehand — before I remembered, before I went looking for it. If I had somehow forgotten that I had an anxiety problem, maybe I wouldn't have noticed anything wrong. Maybe I would have simply gone about my day, feeling perfectly fine.

If you're in the habit of scanning your body and looking for signs of anxiety too, my advice is to stop searching for it. Try to wean yourself off that habit. When you expect to discover that something's wrong with you, you can easily convince your mind that you've found it — even if, in reality, you're perfectly fine.

If you happen to notice that you're truly anxious, that's okay too. Don't sweat it. Just apply the Fu*k Fear Technique and keep on going about your day.

Key insight:

Stop looking for your anxiety. Cultivate an attitude of not being bothered either way.

DAY 12: GET BORED OF ANXIETY

Every magician knows you should *never* reveal your secrets. Why? Because "magic" is just a fragile veneer with little substance. Once you know how a trick works, it stops being magic. It's just boring.

Anxiety is a trick that fools you into thinking it's big and scary, but, just like magic, it has no real substance. It's all smoke and mirrors. There's nothing to it.

I get that now. That truth is finally starting to sink in.

Each day I'm less captivated by my anxious feelings. They don't scare, worry or concern me that much anymore.

Oh, I'm so big and scary.. Blah de blah de blah… Snnnooozzzze! Same old BS!

I'm really not interested in anything my anxiety has to say. Often I forget all about it. I'm not sure if it leaves or if I've just stopped noticing it. Is there a difference?

Other times I notice that it's still there, sulking in the background like a moody teenager, but it's getting easier to ignore.

The less bothered I am by anxiety, the less power it has over me. So I actively cultivate an attitude of *truly not giving a shit* about it.

If I truly didn't care about something, if it really didn't bother me in the slightest, I wouldn't talk about it. I wouldn't ruminate over it and I wouldn't overanalyze it. I would be apathetic and casual about it. I would be bored of it.

The more my anxiety bores me, the freer I feel.

It took me a while to figure out that I was actually experiencing a phenomenon called *habituation*.

Habituation is a natural process that causes our response to frequently repeated stimuli to diminish over time. As we keep encountering the same stimulus over and over again, we grow to accept it. We expect to encounter it, so it doesn't come as a surprise anymore. We simply get used to it.

Here's a little story about habituation that might help you gain a deeper understanding of it.

A story about habituation

You're casually walking in a park one day. Out of the blue, a man walks up to you and starts telling you a story. You quickly realize that it's no ordinary story — it's horrible, grotesque and terrifying.

"Why are you telling me this? This is horrible!" you exclaim. Yet the man keeps telling you his scary story nonetheless.

"Please, be quiet," you plead. And yet he keeps on talking.

You don't want to hear it. It's too awful! So you turn around and start running.

The man refuses to give up. He starts pursuing you. He runs after you, yelling his story louder and louder. He starts catching up.

You run faster. You run as fast as your legs can carry you.

You put your hands over your ears, but he yells even louder.

You begin singing in an effort to drown him out, but you can still hear his voice.

Now he's screaming the story at the top of his lungs. It's too loud. It's deafening!

"How is that even possible?" you ask yourself as you desperately try to get away from him.

You've been running so fast and for so long that your legs feel like they're on fire. Your feet are blistered and bleeding. Your heart is beating so rapidly that it seems like it's about to burst out of your chest. You're gasping for air.

It's too much. Running is too painful. His story couldn't possibly be more horrible than the pain of running, could it?

So you stop running.

The man finally catches up with you — and, sure enough, he goes on telling his horrible story. It's an awful, twisted tale that doesn't seem to have any other purpose besides frightening the life out of you. Your blood boils. Tingles are running down your spine. You've never been more afraid.

After an hour or so, the man finishes his story. "Phew! Finally!" you say. "Now will you please leave me alone?!"

But the man starts telling his story all over again. Your legs are too tired to move this time, so you just stand there, listening to the same tale.

This time, however, it's different. You already know the story. You know what happens. The element of the unknown is gone, so it's less scary.

Another hour passes. The man finishes his story and starts telling it once again.

This time around, you're starting to get bored. It all feels too familiar. What was so frightening at first doesn't faze you at all anymore.

The man continues droning on about this and that. After a while, you just tune him out. Your legs are rested now, so you get up, walk away and simply get on with your day.

The man keeps on following you around though, repeating his story over and over. You stop caring and just let him do whatever. As he goes on and on, you start to drown him out and focus your attention elsewhere. You're not bothered. Mostly, you're just grateful that you're not running anymore.

One day, you look around and notice that the man is gone. "I didn't even notice him leaving!" you think to yourself.

The more we hang out with our anxious, fearful feelings, the less scary they become. As they begin to feel familiar and our nervous system gradually learns that these feelings aren't something to be feared, it gets easier and easier to tune them out and just get on with things. Eventually, these feelings disappear altogether without you even noticing that they're gone.

> **Key insight**
>
> Allow yourself to become bored of anxious sensations. Once you're bored of them, it doesn't matter if they're there or not. You barely even notice them.

THREE WEEKS LATER...

———

Over the past few weeks, I've made remarkable progress. Every day I've been practicing the Fu*k Fear technique — and it works! It really, really works, but…

But it's still a relatively new skill for me. And tomorrow I've got my biggest test yet.

I'm getting married tomorrow. That reality is set in stone.

It's a big wedding. Everyone who is close to me will be there. Watching. I'm not sure if I'm ready for that sort of pressure, but there's no turning back now.

I'm worried that I'm going to be anxious tomorrow. I'm worried that all of this worry about being anxious tomorrow is going to make me anxious tomorrow. I see myself as a messy puddle of sweat at the altar, a ball of anxiety wrapped in a tuxedo, destined to disappoint my new wife on her special day.

What if I have a panic attack in the middle of the ceremony?

Oh, God…

Please, let me hold my shit together…

GETTING MARRIED

"I'M GETTING MARRIED TODAY!" the thought dashes through my brain before I'm even half-awake. It's early morning and I'm staying over at my mom's house in Ireland. It's hard to believe that the big day is *finally* here. It all seems a bit surreal and mildly unnerving.

I get out of bed, intending to grab a sandwich before I start preparing for the ceremony. I take a couple of steps and then, suddenly, I feel an instant rush of anxiety.

WHOOOOOOSH!

My stomach drops and my heart feels like it's going to burst out of my chest.

"Okay, Richy. You know what to do."

I sit down on the bed, compose myself, think, "Fu*k it" and drop the struggle. By now, I'm very familiar with the technique, so I allow the muscles in my body to relax completely. I soften my mind, diffusing any fears and worries.

Next, I bring my anxious feelings home — and I'm surprised at how easy it is. I'm strangely happy to embrace my anxiety. In truth, a part of me is glad that my anxiety is here. It's been such a big part of my life, so it feels only right for it to show up on my big day as well! I wouldn't want that side of me to miss the experience. So I honestly, warmly, deeply welcome it to me.

Warmth. Love. Acceptance. Compassion. I feel a softness pulse out from my stomach. My anxiety starts to ebb away. As it does so, I give it full permission to come back whenever it wishes. It's going to be okay. I'm going to be okay. I know that now. I can feel it deep in my bones.

This is one of the most important and exciting days of my life. Who knows what I'm going to feel as I marry the love of my life? Afraid, vulnerable, nervous maybe? But also excited, delighted and loved.

Whatever I feel, these are *my* feelings. They're an essential part of today's experience. I don't want to spend a single moment of my wedding denying who I am. Instead, I want to spend this day *fully experiencing* who I am. All of it. Anxiety and nerves included. Who isn't nervous on their wedding day anyway?

I shift my focus away from what I don't want and onto what I do want — which is a truly special day for Ali.

How did the day go, you ask?

It was magic. Ali looked stunning. The ceremony was beautiful. Tears of joy were shed. It snowed. And we all partied into the morning hours.

Anxiety? What anxiety? I was too busy feeling like the luckiest man on Earth!

Wedding Bliss!

FAQ'S

Here are some common FAQs for the Fu*k Fear technique.

"Why is my anxiety taking so long to go away?"

It's important that you allow your anxiety to stay for as long as it needs to. Remember, that's *your* anxiety. You've created it. It has every right to be there. It naturally takes time for anxious feelings to dissolve. It can be a matter of hours, or it can be a matter of days. Whatever's the case, make some room for your feelings and allow them to be processed in their own way.

"Why is my anxiety getting stronger?"

Like the tide, anxiety and fear tend to ebb and flow. Sometimes they're stronger and at other times, not so much. This is the nature of anxiety. Sure, it can be frustrating, but the best thing you can do is give those anxious sensations space to do as they please. In time, they'll calm down and fade away.

"But I still feel afraid?!"

It's okay to feel fear. Fear is a natural and normal feeling. It's only a problem if you turn it into one. The moment you try to free yourself from your fear, you start resisting it. Resistance, in any form, does not end fear. It prolongs it.

"This is very uncomfortable!"

That's okay. You can handle discomfort. You've probably been uncomfortable for years. You're used to it. Besides, I'm sure that you can think of many things that are a lot more uncomfortable than anxiety is. Giving birth, breaking your leg, scalding yourself... The list goes on. The bottom line is that the feeling of anxiety is less than ideal, but it's not intolerable.

"But I don't like this feeling!"

Who says that you have to like your feelings? It's okay if you don't like the feeling of being anxious, but that doesn't mean that you have to fight it. If you had a car you didn't particularly like, would you pick up a baseball bat and smash it to pieces? Nope. That would only add more suffering to the suffering that you're already experiencing.

"But I WANT it to leave!"

Of course you'd rather that the feeling wasn't there. That's perfectly understandable. But these anxious feelings *are* here. Fighting that reality only adds further stress and suffering to your existence.

"But it's so intense!"

Yes. But that's all it is. It's just an intense feeling. The pounding heart, the tight stomach, the jittery legs, the sweating, the rapid breathing — that's what you feel after a quick jog. You aren't concerned then, are you? So why should you be worried now?

"But I feel so vulnerable!"

Of course you do! If you're embracing anxiety or fear, you're bound to feel vulnerable — especially for the first few times. That's a given. You're stepping on uncertain ground. It comes with the territory. Besides, feeling vulnerable can be a good sign. It means that you're pushing yourself outside your comfort zone and growing as a person.

"But I'm not brave enough, strong enough, confident enough to handle those feelings!"

You *are* brave enough. Suffering with anxiety every day, you've had to confront fears that most people never have to deal with. If that's not bravery, I don't know what is.

"But I just want to feel in control!"

When did you ever really have control over your feelings? Never. You've never been able to control your feelings. In any case, if you think that your feelings are indeed controllable, what happens when you inevitably do lose control? You're more likely to panic and feel out of control! It's better to just let go of the idea of emotional control altogether. You're not a robot. You're a human being. Embrace your human feelings.

"But this should not be happening!"

This is happening. This is your reality. Once something has occurred, fighting that reality won't help. You can choose to accept this fact or reject it, but reality will stubbornly remain the same either way.

"But I didn't ask for this!"

That's right. You didn't ask for anxiety. But it is here nonetheless. Resisting that fact is completely useless.

"Why do I have to do this now? Can't I just go into a corner and hide? I'll start tomorrow, I promise!"

Really? What's going to be so different about tomorrow? Why do we always imagine that in the future, we're going to be braver, more confident, and finally have our shit together? You've put this off long enough.

"It worked! I've applied the technique and stopped feeling anxious! Will it work every time?"

No. If your anxiety does subside after applying the Fu*k Fear technique, you should treat it as a mere bonus. Sometimes your anxiety will leave quickly and at other times, it'll require some patience. In any case, you should try and remove your expectations. Don't put pressure on your anxiety to leave. If it does leave, that's great — but if it refuses to go away immediately, you should let it do its own thing and embrace it anyway.

"How will I know when I'm over it?"

It'll happen when anxiety stops being a problem for you. You may still feel anxious from time to time, but it won't concern you as much or get in the way of you living your life to the fullest.

"Why don't I ever feel completely relaxed and at ease?"

Nobody ever feels 100% at ease. Even when we feel relaxed, happy and content, our brain keeps scanning our environment for potential dangers. Consequently, in the back of our minds, there's always a subtle sense of unease — whether we notice it or not. If you're lucky, you might spend the rest of your life with only 5% of your inner world being anxious and alert, but you must be prepared to have *some* uncomfortable feelings. What's important isn't the uncomfortable feelings themselves, but rather your reaction to them.

"But I don't want to feel discomfort!"

Ask yourself: how much discomfort could you possibly find acceptable?

What about 1% of discomfort? Would you be fine with feeling 1% of discomfort?

What about 5% of discomfort?

Or 15%?

Or 50%?

At what point does it become unacceptable?

You decide whether or not it's acceptable. It's a simple choice. You can choose how much discomfort you're willing to tolerate. If you want, you can choose to be 100% comfortable with feeling 100% of discomfort. The boundary to what you accept is the boundary to your freedom!

"If you are afraid of the discomforts of life, you will resist them and turn them into suffering." — Pema Chodron

"How much mental space should I give to my anxiety?"

The more space you give it, the better. Why not give it *all* the space? Then build some extra mental space in your mind, and give it that too!

"Can't I just keep on resisting my anxiety?

Resisting anxiety truly is banging your head against the wall of reality. By resisting our experiences, we amplify our discomfort and increase our suffering. When it comes to fear, the only way out is through.

"Bringing my feelings home feels awkward!"

Sure, bringing your feelings home can feel awkward if you're not used to doing it. It's like meeting an old friend: initially, talking to them might feel a little forced, awkward and inauthentic, but soon you get comfortable with each other and it all starts flowing naturally again. Just keep at it. With each passing day, embracing your feelings will go more and more smoothly.

"But I want to feel confident and wonderful, not vulnerable and sensitive!"

True confidence is allowing yourself to feel the full spectrum of your emotions. Sometimes you may feel strong, loud and powerful. At other times, you might feel quiet, insecure and scared. All of these feelings are you, and all of them are absolutely okay.

"But I'll die if I let anxiety run over me!"

Then allow yourself to die. Go ahead! You won't die.

"If I don't fight my anxiety, won't I just spiral into an anxious mess?"

You might feel like you have to keep your anxious feelings dammed up, or else there'll be a flood. But if you hadn't dammed them up in the first place, there wouldn't have been a flood! It's like opening a bottle of sparkling water: if you do it slowly and release the pressure bit by bit, you're safe.

"If I accept anxiety, won't it just stay?"

We tend to believe that if we accept things just as they are, without trying to change them, they'll always be with us. Anxiety and fear are like gaseous substances. If you allow them to just be there, they'll eventually dissipate on their own.

"But my anxious feelings are wrong!"

Says who? There's no right or wrong way to feel. If you feel bad, that doesn't always mean that there's something wrong with you or that you did something wrong. Anxiety, fear and sadness are all uncomfortable emotions, but they aren't wrong in and of themselves.

"I'm too tired to do this!"

At times, bringing your anxiety home does require a lot of effort. But in the long run, it's a lot easier than spending years trying to block your emotions out.

"How do I know if it's working?"

You'll know that it's working when you feel more at ease, calm and centered, even while still being anxious. In time, the anxious feelings themselves will dissolve too.

"I'm not strong enough!"

Bullsh*t! Living with anxiety and fear every day requires inner strength and resolve that most people never tap into. Trust me, you're a lot stronger than you think.

For extra tools, guidance and support go to: https://ffear.co

---

PART 3

Moving Forward

AKA How I learned to embrace life

STEP OUTSIDE YOUR COMFORT ZONE

———

I'm no longer a slave to my anxiety. It's wonderful to be able to exist in the moment without feeling overwhelmed or zoned-out, but I still have a ways to go. My wounds are healing, yet they're still tender. My resilience is increasing, yet my nerves are still sensitive. My confidence is improving, yet my self-esteem is still in tatters. Anxiety has played such a huge part in my life for so long that I feel a little lost without it.

How do I pick up the broken pieces of my life?

How do I start living again?

How do I feel present, open and real?

How do I step forward into life?

I'm a bird that's been trapped in a cage for so long that it's forgotten how to fly.

I'm tempted to play it safe and stay inside my little, predictable bubble — just me, my family and my web design business. But deep down, I'm thinking, "Fu*k that." Feeling safe and comfortable won't be my prime motivation for existing. I want to live again. I want adventure, playfulness, novelty, danger, surprise, fun, the unknown. Life is short. There's a big world out there and I've already lost plenty of years playing it safe. What's the point of learning how to make peace with my fear if I don't use that skill to engage in life?

Besides, now that I'm making good progress, the worst mistake I could possibly make is falling back into my old routine. My skills are still pretty fresh, so it's imperative that I continue strengthening them. I must keep moving forward — or else all of this will have been for nothing. I need to keep looking under the bed, reminding myself that the monsters aren't real. The more I do it, the more I'll increase my resilience and build confidence in my capacity to handle whatever comes my way.

Like a man possessed, I take every opportunity to flex my Fu*k Fear muscle. I start random conversations with checkout attendants. I get friendly with my neighbours, having regular conversations over the back fence. I join a local yoga studio and a CrossFit gym. I reconnect with old friends and seek new ones. I finally allow Ali to host social get-togethers at our house. After a few months, I close my web design business and start pursuing a new venture — one that's way more risky, but also way more fun, rewarding and enjoyable.

Each day I do something, however small, that pushes me outside my comfort zone. Each day I step forward into uncertainty and doubt. Each day I practice the Fu*k Fear technique — and it supports me the whole way through.

Here's how you can use the Fu*k Fear technique to help you move forward into your own less anxious life:

Step 1: Fu*k fear and step into uncertainty.

Of course, the idea of stepping outside of your comfort zone is inherently anxiety-inducing. There's so much uncertainty, doubt and worry about everything. How will I cope? What if I fall apart? What if I don't know what to do? What if the sky collapses right on top of my head? Your mind might start listing reasons why you should just stay in your safe bubble, hide and play it safe.

We develop all kinds of ways to stay in our comfort zone. We wall ourselves off from danger, avoid difficult conversations, difficult projects and any situations where we might flop on our faces.

But in order to move forward in life, we need to drop our guard and step outside our comfort zone.

When you feel *any* resistance against stepping outside your comfort zone think, "Fu*k it!" and drop your concerns. Drop your guard and drop your need for control.

Refuse to get caught up in all the reasons why you should play it safe. You don't need to pay them any heed. Soften your mind, soften your resistance.

Trust that you can deal with whatever comes up. Trust in your ability to ride the wave of your moment-to-moment experience. Trust in your ability to make it all up as you go along. All the wisdom and knowledge you need to persevere is already there, inside you. You've managed to survive up to this point in your life, so chances of surviving even further are all in your favour. Whatever happens, remember that you're capable of dealing with it. You don't have to hide anymore.

Step 2: Just bring it home!

Whatever you experience as you step outside your comfort zone, just bring it all home to you. The good and the bad. Embrace it all. Allow yourself to feel what you feel. Studies show that people who try to suppress their fear before giving a public speech not only feel more anxious, but also have higher heart rates.

If you feel fear, that's fine. Not a problem. Why does feeling sensations of fear have to be a problem anyway?

We tend to think that life would be better without fear. But without it, people would be constantly stepping out in front of traffic without any hesitation. Your first kiss would be a non-event, forgotten in a split second. Roller coasters, haunted houses and scary movies wouldn't exist. No one would climb dangerous mountains because why would they? What would be the point in doing that? Why would you do that if you're not conquering any fears?

When I asked Ali to marry me, I was terrified — but it was easily one of the best days of my life. During the births of my kids, I was riddled with concern and worry, and yet words can't express how special those moments were. Fear *can* be serious and grim, but if you're safe (and you *are* safe), fear can be energy, excitement, drive, tingles down your spine and jitters during your first date. It can be one of the greatest pleasures in the world.

Besides, stepping outside your comfort zone generally means allowing yourself to feel vulnerable. That's just a fact of life.

I used to detest feeling vulnerable. It made me feel weak, exposed and insecure. But I've learned to find the deliciousness in it. Being vulnerable offers me **relief from having to hide from my true self**. It gifts me the simplicity of just being who I am — without having to change a thing.

Stepping outside your comfort zone can be scary, but it can also be fun, adventurous, spontaneous, fresh, playful and exciting. It can be one of the most beautiful experiences in the world.

When we drop our guard, all situations become more spontaneous, open and unfettered. Life feels a little bit more adventurous. For me, this is the essence of freedom and feeling truly alive.

Bring your vulnerability home to you. Allow it to exist. Find the deliciousness in it.

Our greatest strength

Being open to our vulnerability does not make us weak. Far from it. In fact, it might just be one of our greatest strengths. **It allows us to do all of the things that we've been too afraid to do before.**

You're reading this book, for example. As best I could, I tried to open up and show my vulnerable side — my weaknesses, my worries, my struggles, my warts, my pain. My hope is that this will make you feel just a little bit more comfortable with your own personal struggles. If it does, then all of this will have been worth it.

On the other hand, you might just as well think that I'm a crackpot weirdo and that this book is the biggest joke on planet Earth. I can't control your reaction and I don't have the slightest clue how you feel about me. But I can be comfortable with this uncertainty.

The point is, I'm not letting that uncertainty hold me back from telling you the truth of who I am and how I feel. Embracing my vulnerability has allowed me to overcome my fear of writing this book.

When you're no longer threatened by your inner world, an amazing thing happens. It's hard to put it into words, but when you realize that nothing in your inner world can stop you, the outer world becomes less scary. You feel… free.

A deeper connection

How can we connect with others in an intimate way if we avoid being vulnerable?

When you come from a place of honesty, people see that. They really do. They value and respect you for being brave enough to be yourself. **When you accept your own vulnerability, others accept it too.**

By opening up to your vulnerable feelings, you come into your life from a place that better reflects the real, true you. This allows for deeper connections with others, more nuanced experiences and a deeper insight into who you are as a person.

Me... "I'm NOT vulnerable" (kind of a fake me)

Me... "I'm always vulnerable" (the REAL me)

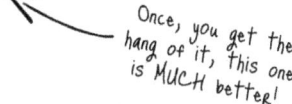

Once, you get the hang of it, this one is MUCH better!

Taking action

What's most important is that you take action. Try doing something every day that gently pushes you towards your own vulnerability. See it as essential training.

Perhaps you could talk to a stranger. Or you could drive your car to the corner of the street. Or you could go swimming in a public pool. Or you could have a short walk around the park by yourself. Or you could join a local fitness club.

Perhaps you could find something you've been delaying for a while and lean into the discomfort of it. Or face a scary project you've been trying not to think about. Or have a difficult conversation you've been afraid of having.

The possibilities are truly endless.

The more you practice, the less daunting stepping into vulnerability becomes — until, eventually, **you start to enjoy the thrill of it.**

The key is to fully support yourself, no matter what. It doesn't matter if you slip up, fall down, get scared or get lost — as long as you always have your own back, you're going to be just fine.

Open up to discovery

Each time you step forward into life, be proud of yourself for that achievement.

As you keep on conquering new challenges, you might be surprised by what you discover about yourself. Who knows? You might find out that you love the limelight, that you secretly crave danger and that you were a complete extrovert all along. Or perhaps you'll discover that you really savor deep, quiet conversations, cuddling up on the sofa with a good book and being on your own. Or you might find that your true personality is a mixture of both of these aspects.

Until you drop your guard, step into vulnerability and warmly embrace all of your feelings, you won't really know… but isn't it exciting to find out?

STEPPING OFF THE GAS

Stepping outside your comfort zone is the key to freedom — but at the same time, there's no need to rush here. Feel free to go at a pace and speed that is *right for you*. Take small steps and allow your confidence to grow naturally.

The key is to **honor your limits** as you move forward

We're all born with different levels of resilience to stress. We all have our unique, personal "boiling points" — certain levels of stress that cause us to feel sensitized and edgy. What's too much for us might be fine for others. It can be really helpful to get a feel for our own stress capacity.

After testing my limits for a few weeks, I've found out that they're by no means impressive. Actually, my tolerance bar is pretty low. 2 or 3 cups of coffee can turn me into a wired mess. Driving a car for more than 4 hours straight does that too. The same goes for working on a computer for more than 4 hours without a break, or two late nights in a row, or any social occasion that lasts for more than 6 hours. But as I learn to look after myself better, I do find that my resilience is vastly improving.

Here are some guidelines I try to follow:

- Take a break of at least 5 minutes for every 25 minutes of screen time.
- Avoid coffee after 3 P.M. No more than one cup of coffee per day. And take a few days off coffee altogether from time to time.
- If possible, have a nap instead of coffee as a pick-me-up.
- Try not to skip more than one day of yoga.
- Go to bed at a reasonable hour and try to get at least 7 hours of sleep.
- Consume some healthy, fresh food daily.
- Drink alcohol very moderately if you do drink it at all.

- Spend a few hours in nature at least once a week.
- Take magnesium daily.
- Give yourself some cave time if and when you need it.
- Have some quality alone time every few days.
- Avoid getting too run-down or tired in general.

It's ridiculous how often I don't follow my own advice. I get cocky and start disrespecting my limits. "It's fine. I'm on a roll! I'll just grab another cup of coffee and bash out a few more hours on the computer!" Later I find myself lying on the sofa, buzzed, tired and sensitive. I wonder how many times I need to learn the same lesson over and over again before it really sinks in. But I'm getting better at it, and that's all that matters.

We all have our own personal limits. They're not a sign of weakness and they're not something to be ashamed of. It's okay if you don't want to party until 4 in the morning. It's okay if you want to go to bed early with a warm cup of chamomile tea. There's no shame in that whatsoever.

Observe your reactions to different situations. Notice what works for you and what doesn't. Do you feel more anxious when you're tired? What is the impact of daily screen time on your emotional state? Yes, there's a fair bit of trial and error involved here, but if you're paying attention to how you feel, it becomes a great deal clearer pretty soon.

Once you're aware of your limits, be clear and honest with yourself. Try to respect and honor your limits as best you can. Most importantly, don't judge yourself if you end up overstepping the line from time to time. We all do it!

Exhaustion

Let's talk about something that's closely related to anxiety — exhaustion.

Most people don't realize just how exhausting being anxious can be. The constant worry, the stress, the strain, thoughts racing a mile a minute... Everything's turned up to eleven.

That's the thing with anxiety: you're exhausted, yet you don't feel tired. You feel *wired*. You're so out of it that your body doesn't even register how tired you really are. You've gone so far past exhaustion that all the safety checks that indicate a desperate need for rest have blown their fuses. You're like a wounded soldier, stumbling around the battlefield, not even aware that you're missing an arm. The more exhausted and burnt-out you are, the less likely you are to recognize that you need to rest and recuperate. Some people spend their whole lives in such a state without even knowing it.

Not only that, but exhaustion is a primary trigger for anxiety. If I'm feeling sensitive or anxious, nine times out of ten it's because I've been overdoing it, working too hard or not getting enough sleep. Exhaustion puts us in a sensitized state. We become less resilient to stress and more prone to feeling overwhelmed. In this state, molehills can feel like mountains. Before we know it, we're stuck in a downward spiral of feeling anxious because we're tired — which makes us more tired, which makes us more anxious. To break this cycle, it's essential to have some proper rest once in a while.

Look after your marbles

Imagine your energy levels as marbles in a jar. Each marble is a unit of energy. If you take good care of yourself, you wake up each morning with a jar that is chock-full of marbles. Every action throughout the day uses up some of those marbles. Ideally, you still have a few of them left in the jar at the end of the day.

However, if you're sensitive to anxiety, every action requires a little more effort than usual — which means that you run out of marbles a great deal quicker. Brushing your teeth? Two marbles. Making yourself a sandwich? Five marbles. Going to the shop to pick up some groceries? Ten marbles. Getting some work done at the office?.. Forget it, you barely have any marbles left!

If you notice that you feel more tired than usual, or that your capacity to perform simple, everyday tasks is lower than normal, or that you aren't as sharp as you normally tend to be, take that as a note that your marbles are likely to be running low.

Rather than drifting through life like a half-engaged zombie, take some much-needed time to refill your marbles. You might need a few hours, or you might need a couple of days. Just give yourself as much time as you can possibly muster. Once your energy is restored, you'll realize that it's been more than worth it.

How can you know that you need some rest?

Usually, all it takes is listening to your feelings. If you just pay attention to them, you'll know when you need solace and comfort. You'll know when you need some space and quality alone time. You'll know when you need company or a warm hug from a loved one. If you really listen to what your feelings are trying to tell you, you can deal with them while they're still nothing more than whispers — as a result, your feelings don't have to scream at you to get what they need.

If, however, you've gone past mere tiredness and stepped into the realm of exhaustion, you might not even recognize that you're in desperate need of some rest. If that's the case, it's best if you force yourself to take a break, even if you don't feel like it. Usually, after a day or two, once your body regains its balance, you'll really feel the full weight of your exhaustion. Take that as a good sign. You're moving in the right direction!

Here are some of my favorite strategies that might help you refill your marble jar too:

1. Take a nap

I'm a huge fan of napping. It really does me wonders. If you feel tired during the day or if you've missed out on sleep, take a 20-minute nap. It can have a huge impact on your mood and energy levels.

2. Get a good night's sleep

Over the years, I've learned that I really need my sleep. Just one night of interrupted sleep can knock me off.

Sleep seems like an obvious human need, but for some reason, we think it's cool to rebel against it. We live in a *I'll-sleep-when-I'm-dead* culture. That's far from the right thing to do. You need to sleep to stay calm and sane! Chronic sleep deprivation elevates your cortisol levels, which leaves you more prone to stress. Getting adequate sleep, on the other hand, lowers them significantly.

Think about how much sleep you're getting. If you get less than 7 hours of sleep a night, consider rearranging your schedule in a way that would allow you to sleep longer. I find that 7-8 hours of sleep work perfectly for me.

If falling asleep is a challenge for you, it can be helpful to establish a bedtime ritual. Go to bed and wake up at around the same time every day, and start slowing down at least an hour before bedtime. It takes time for your body and mind to unwind, so try and ease into it.

3. Cave time

One of my favorite ways to rest is to hide away in my cave for a while. We all need a safe bubble, obscured from the rest of the world, where we can do whatever we want — without any judgement or responsibilities. All humans need space to just *be*.

My cave time always starts with me giving myself full permission to do absolutely nothing. This is a special time for me. It's essential for my well-being. No working, no planning, no setting or achieving goals, no need to be anything but my lazy, tired self. I allow myself to just do whatever I feel like doing.

Here are 10 things I like to do during my personal cave time:

1. Lying on the sofa with a blanket and binge-watching TV shows.
2. Lazy, silly, playful yoga. Just moving my body in whichever way I see fit — usually with some music in the background
3. Taking a nice, long bath.
4. Going to the cinema by myself.
5. Snoozing.
6. Wearing my cozy clothes all day. Ideally, these are a bit sloppy and not suitable for the general public.
7. *Me party!* Time to put some music on and dance around the house.
8. Embracing my inner nerd and indulging in some computer games or sci-fi movies.

9. Did someone say take-away food?
10. Sitting on the sofa with a warm cup of tea and enjoying the peace and quiet.

If possible, I try to get at least a few hours of cave time when I'm feeling run-down — hopefully, more. You may have to rearrange your life a little or ask for some support so you can take some proper time out.

During your cave time, just do whatever you want to do. If you want to wrap yourself into a ball with multiple blankets, hang upside down and chant "om" for 5 hours, go for it! Your self-care doesn't have to look like anyone else's. **There are no rules here**. Do whatever feels right for *you*.

Cave time is very different from running away from anxiety. It comes from a place of love. It recognizes your core needs and honors them. There's absolutely no shame in needing some cave time.

4. Lower your standards

If you notice that your batteries are running low, aim for small victories. Accept that you're going to get less done that day. You don't have to give up your responsibilities completely, but it's a good idea to lower your goals for the time being. Maybe you can do 50% of what you've hoped to get done and still get away with it?

5. Put yourself first

When was the last time you did something nice for yourself just for the sake of it? Most of us don't do it nearly enough — and boy, do we miss out.

Try putting yourself first and doing something nice for yourself at least once a day. This is a fantastic way of letting yourself take a well-deserved break and accepting that you're worthy of self-care.

"Isn't this a bit self-indulgent?"

Absolutely not.

I know that feeling guilty can be a major deterrent when it comes to taking a rest. Sitting around often makes us feel lazy or like we're not getting the most out of life. Our culture frowns on any sort of laziness. Why? What's wrong with being lazy for a couple of days? Being lazy can be delicious if we really allow ourselves to savor it.

After a good rest, you'll be much more productive, alert and focused. Life will just flow smoother. By taking care of ourselves, we can all become better fathers, mothers, lovers, sisters, brothers and friends. Imagine if the whole world did this. How much happier would everyone be?

Besides, if you don't rest when you're tired, you'll burn out and will be forced to take a rest anyway. Our bodies have ways of getting what they need — whether we want them to or not.

 Key insight

Honor your limits. Exhaustion is a primary trigger for anxiety. Listen to your feelings to know when you need to rest. Make rest your top priority.

FU*K SETBACKS!

———

After three months of making great progress, I have my first setback. It's a big one and, if I'm completely honest, it's all my fault. I got a little too cocky and overdid it. I committed to a tight deadline on a project that resulted in too many coffee-fuelled late nights back to back. Rather than taking some time out and having a rest, I just kept on pushing. "I'll be fine!" I kept telling myself. Sure, if being "fine" means hiding under the duvet, feeling devastated, gutted and extra sensitive to anxiety.

After all those weeks of amazing progress, relapsing hurts. It *really* hurts. I'm racked with worry and stress. Dark thoughts keep spinning around in my head:

"Why did I get my stupid hopes up?"

"I'm back to square one!"

"I'll never be free from anxiety!"

"Perhaps other people can break free, but I sure can't!"

What all of these thoughts really boil down to is fear. A deep-seated fear that I've been fooling myself all along, that I simply don't have what it takes to break free, that I'm doomed to live a life of never-ending anxiety.

I can tell you right now that **those fears are all bullsh*t.**

If you're going to get better, you have to push yourself. If you push yourself, you're going to fall. If you're not falling, you're not pushing hard enough. **Falling is a necessary part of getting better.** Setbacks are an essential part of the journey to freedom from anxiety. You will have setbacks.

The good news is that you already have the perfect tool to deal with setbacks right in your back pocket. Yep, you guessed it — the Fu*k Fear technique works for that too. Here's how you can use it to get over a setback:

Step 1: Think, "Fu*k it" and drop your concern.

You've had a setback. So what? These things happen. It's all part of the journey. **Everyone** fails, makes mistakes and gets it wrong sometimes. We're not alone in our imperfection.

Yes, setbacks are upsetting. I'm sure you'd prefer it if they didn't happen, but they do. You can't change that reality. Resisting that fact only increases your suffering. Just like fear and anxiety, you don't need to take a setback seriously. Think, "Fu*k it!" and shrug any concerns off as best you can. The more you can brush them off, the better.

Not taking a setback too seriously is really the key factor here. I had a few setbacks, but because I took each one less seriously than the one before, I was less frustrated and rebounded much more quickly.

Step 2: Just bring it home!

Who shows up in your corner when you first have a setback? Is it your anger or your self-compassion?

When we fail, most of us focus on the failure. We're hurting, but we don't feel compassion towards our own pain. Instead, we feel guilt, shame and confusion. There's a crucial difference between feeling like we've failed and feeling like we deserve compassion for the hurt caused by our failure.

We need to recognize this difference. We need to stop for a breath or two and acknowledge that our pain deserves a kind, caring response. Setbacks suck. They feel devastating. You're hurting inside. **It's imperative that you support yourself through this tough time.**

Accept that it's happened and forgive yourself fully. Remind yourself that there's no such thing as a straightforward path to freedom. **You're making progress and that's all that matters.**

Path to freedom

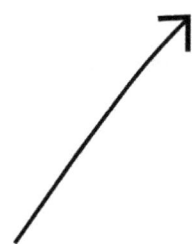

What people think it looks like

What it REALLY looks like

Go big on self care

During a setback, it's a good idea to truly go big on self-care. Perhaps you can cozy up in bed and just be lazy for a while? Perhaps you can hide in your cave? Would cuddling a loved one make you feel a tiny bit better? Listen to your feelings and your needs. Treat yourself kindly and you'll bounce back much quicker.

FU*K WORRY!

As a species, we simply love to worry.

We worry about disease, injury and death.

We worry about that suspicious mole on our shoulder.

We worry that the airplane might crash.

We worry that we'll look silly and be judged harshly.

We worry that our life isn't good enough, that we're missing out on all the fun, that we're not happy enough, special enough, not enough in general.

We worry that we'll run out of money and live on the streets, or that someone's going to break into our apartment, or that the door handle in the public toilet isn't clean.

The list goes on, and on, and on. There's an endless supply of potential worries in our anxious minds.

Where do these worries come from? Mostly, they come from our imagination. Our minds like to imagine potential threats to ensure that we stay alert. Over millions of years of evolution, our brains have evolved into little worry machines that pop unexpected *what if?* scenarios into our heads almost endlessly throughout the day.

What if this terrible thing happens? What if that terrible thing happens?

Experts estimate that we have roughly 60,000 thoughts every day. Most of them are complete waffle, nonsense, white noise that's not really worth paying much attention to — but when we have a worrying thought, it jumps out at us and grabs our attention. We take it seriously and act as if something bad truly might happen to us.

"This elevator is going to crash and I'm going to die a horrible death!"

BANG!

Just like that, you feel the emotional kick in your body. Your stomach sinks, your fight-or-flight response is triggered and you're suddenly hooked. The emotional response fools you into thinking that the threat is real.

The more emotional these thoughts make us feel, the more easily we take the bait. Rather than passing through our minds unnoticed, worries get stuck as we ruminate and obsess over them — and then it's us who get stuck in a state of constant worry. We become afraid to let go of worry in case our world falls apart. We feel as though all of this worrying is somehow keeping us safe. But our worries only keep us safe long enough to worry some more. Eventually, we lose the ability to be playful, light-hearted, loose, carefree and instead end up trapped in a straitjacket of worry.

What most of us don't realize is that all the time spent worrying that something terrible is going to happen to us has *already* caused something terrible to happen. It's caused us to be trapped in a state of constant worry!

So what can we do about our worries?

Well, we could try to resolve each worry one by one. But the problem is that this doesn't really work. First of all, it would take us forever. Secondly, it would most likely be impossible. And finally, it would be pointless, as another worry would soon take the place of the previous one (haven't you noticed that the world is full of things to worry about?).

Alternatively, we could try to alleviate our fear by mentally rationalizing against our worries.

Perhaps we could make a list of our worries and a second list of counterarguments. But this is just another form of arguing with ourselves — and, as we've already learned, fighting ourselves is never a good idea.

I tried both of these techniques and, if anything, they made my worries worse. I became too self-critical, too self-conscious and spent too much time being trapped in a spiral of having thoughts about thoughts. I find that trying to use your mind to fix your mind often just ends up creating an extra layer of stress.

Besides, even if you did manage to get rid of a worry for a short time, what would you do when the worry came back? You'd most likely feel like a failure, spiral out of control and become even more worried.

Instead of battling your worries, you can use the Fu*k Fear technique to accept and alleviate them. This technique works wonders here too, as anxiety and worry often go hand in hand.

Step 1: Think, "Fu*k it" and let go.

Just like fear and anxiety, most of your worries are pure fiction.

Think about it. Is whatever you're worrying about happening right now? Is it true now, at this very moment?

The reason I ask is this: 99% of our worries are just anticipation — and nothing else.

We all do this.

I might worry that I'm going to crumble to pieces on the shop floor. Is it happening right now? No.

I might worry that the plane I'm flying in is going to crash. Is it crashing right at this moment? No.

I might worry that I'm going to get eaten by a shark. But do I see a shark in the water? No.

I might worry that everybody hates me. But are they being mean to me right now? No. Actually, everyone's quite nice to me (we'd worry a lot less about what people think of us if we realized how seldom they do).

The truth is that we rarely encounter our worries in real life. Generally, you'll find that right now, at this point in time, nothing scary is happening to you. You're not in danger.

Look around you.

Are you in danger right at this moment?

Is something scary actually happening to you?

Is your life in danger right now?

Probably not.

Most of our worries aren't real. Most of our worries are simply thoughts conjured up by our creative minds. What we're really afraid of is our own imagination. What scares us is an endless stream of purely imaginary situations. The danger isn't real. It's just a 'pretend' danger (sounds familiar?).

So if something is seriously worrying you, just ask yourself:

"Is it true now, at this very moment?"

And if it isn't, think, "Fu*k it!" and let go.

Just let your worrying thoughts be. We're not trying to get rid of them. In fact, you don't have to do anything about them. The less you do, the better. Simply let go of the temptation to fix, change, get rid of or judge your worrying thoughts.

Remember: you could have worrying thoughts all day long, but if you treated them exactly like you treat the rest of the 60,000 thoughts that you have every day, you'd barely even notice them. They'd slide off you like water off a duck's back. So treat your worrying thoughts just like you'd treat any other random thought that you have throughout the day. You don't need to take it seriously.

Sometimes your worries can be hard to dismiss. Sometimes they just keep on being all up in your face. In such cases, you can imagine them as an irksome bee. If you swat the bee, you'll make it angry and it might sting you — so it's best to just leave it alone. Yes, it's a bit of a nuisance, but if you just ignore it and let it be, it'll eventually fly away.

Step 2: Just bring it home!

Often our worries stir up uncomfortable feelings in us. That's okay. We can just bring our feelings home. We can soothe and nurture our discomfort, just like we've nurtured our fear.

Try not to judge yourself harshly if you do find yourself worrying. It's not your fault. Worrying is completely natural. Just as your mind will never stop thinking, so will your mind never truly stop worrying. Our brains love to worry! It's just how they work.

Once you've successfully embraced your worries, sit back and look at the world around you. It's still there, isn't it? It hasn't fallen apart!

Do you need to take action?

At times, you might find yourself worrying about something that requires action. Perhaps you need to sort out your bills or visit the doctor? If that's the case, try and direct your energy towards doing just that.

If you feel any resistance when trying to take action, I find this tip really helpful: simply focus on the next step that you need to take. Imagine putting a ring around it and only pay attention to what's inside that ring. Let everything else drift into the background.

Fill out the first few lines of your tax form. Pick up the phone and make an appointment with your doctor. Pick a day for dealing with the issue that you're currently facing and put a note in your calendar. Whatever you do, place your entire focus on that one small thing and stop worrying about everything else for a while. The longest journeys are travelled one step at a time.

Whatever you do, don't forget that you're on your side now. That's going to make things a whole lot easier!

What if your worry is real?

If you have something that's really playing on your mind, yet you're unable to do anything about it (for example, if one of your children is sick), it can be helpful to take a 10-minute worry break.

For 10 minutes, allow yourself to sit with the worrying feeling. Notice what it feels like in your body. Does it have a shape? A color? A texture? Where do you feel it most?

Once you've figured it out, gently embrace that feeling. Allow it to come home to you. This can help you alleviate the worrying feeling at least a tiny bit. You may notice that the feeling has shifted and stopped being so intense.

After those 10 minutes are up, just get up and go about your day.

INCREASE YOUR RESILIENCE

We haven't talked about resilience much in this book. Resilience is the amount of stress your body and mind can take before you start feeling sensitized. The good news is that we can take simple steps to improve our resilience. Here are some strategies I use to boost my resilience to stress.

Lay off coffee

We live in a caffeine-fuelled world. Excessive caffeine use has been shown to raise our stress hormone levels, increase anxiety and interfere with our sleep quality. If you're currently in a sensitized state, I strongly suggest taking a break from coffee. As an alternative, you can switch to green tea or a high-quality decaf blend. In a few days, you'll notice the difference.

Over time, as your tolerance and resilience grows, you can start drinking coffee again, but I'd still recommend limiting it to just one cup a day.

"But I love my coffee!"

So do I, but I love not feeling anxious more! The discomfort of not drinking coffee is a lot less uncomfortable than the discomfort caused by anxiety. Besides, within a week or so, your body will get used to the absence of caffeine and you'll feel much better for it.

Get sweaty with some cardio exercise

Any exercise that gets your heart rate up is beneficial when it comes to anxiety. Exercise in general improves your range of tolerance, releases pent-up stress and burns off cortisol.

Jogging is a good place to start. It's free, you already know how to do it and it can be done anywhere. I have a sneaky suspicion that a lot of runners are secretly anxiety sufferers. However, you should start slowly in order to prevent injury. Jog for 5 minutes at first and then build up from there.

Try doing yoga

I love, love, love yoga. I've been doing it for nearly 20 years and it's transformed my life in more ways than I thought possible. I can't recommend it highly enough. Keep in mind though that while some improvement is felt immediately, the real benefits kick in once you've done it consistently over a longer period of time.

If you're interested in trying it out, I suggest dedicating one month to yoga. Join a local studio or watch classes on YouTube. Try to do some form of yoga at least 5 days a week for one month. Consistency is key. Each new day builds on the previous one. At the end of the month, see how you feel. What benefits have you noticed? Are you sleeping better? Are you feeling more grounded? More comfortable in your own skin? Happier? Generally, if you commit to it for a full month, the benefits are so obvious that there's no turning back.

Walk in nature

Fresh air, gentle exercise, feeling connected to nature. What's not to love?

There's a peace and stillness you get from nature that you can't get anywhere else. Nature doesn't judge you. It just is — and it lets you be who you are too. I usually try to drag my family out for a walk in a Scottish forest at least once a week. It always proves to be time well spent and I start to get cranky if I don't get my nature fix.

Drink more water

Water can make a huge difference to your well-being! Every organ requires water in order to do its job well — and this includes our brain too. If we're dehydrated, we can become a lot more sensitive to anxiety and stress.

I try to carry a water bottle around with me everywhere I go and take small sips from it throughout the day. I recommend that you increase your water intake for a couple of days and see if it has an impact on how you feel. It sure has for me.

Eat more real food

Nutrition advice is often unnecessarily complicated. I prefer to keep it simple. So here's my advice in four words: eat more real food. That's it. Eat more fresh fruit and vegetables. Eat the sort of food your grandmother would've made. Honestly, that's all you need to know when it comes to nutrition.

If you want to go a bit further though, you can try laying off gluten for a week or so. If you find that you start feeling better after the week is over, you may have a gluten intolerance. Lots of people feel better off gluten. I feel better off gluten. It's definitely worth a try.

You can try cutting dairy out of your diet too. As we grow older, we're more likely to suffer from lactose intolerance. Again, simply give it a week and see how you feel.

Take a magnesium supplement

I'd say that this is an absolutely essential step towards a considerably less anxious life. Magnesium is the secret sauce for managing your anxiety. If I meet anyone who is anxious, I always recommend them magnesium.

Magnesium does wonders for our nervous system. It helps us relax and enables us to feel less sensitized. Barry McDonagh from *Dare* recommends 250 mg of magnesium daily. Keep in mind though that the type of magnesium you buy is important: choose magnesium citrate, hydroxyapatite or gluconate. On the other hand, magnesium carbonate, sulfate, aspartate or oxide should be avoided, as they don't work as well. Do a little research before getting yourself some magnesium. If you have any concerns, it's best to consult a doctor before taking any supplements.

Give CBD oil a try

CBD is the new boy in town and it's making a big impact for good reasons. CBD oil can work wonders for anxiety. However, you should keep in mind that the quality of the oil differs depending on the brand, so you should find a trustworthy supplier before trying it out. High-quality CBD oil can be a little expensive, but the investment is worth it if it makes a difference. Give it a month or so and see if it works for you.

• • •

These strategies are all worth trying out. I suggest picking one at a time and focusing on it for a week or two to see if you notice any difference. One thing's for sure though: they've definitely made a difference for me.

QUICK FIXES

―――

Sometimes we just need a quick fix — something simple, fast and effective to help blow off a little steam. Thankfully, our bodies have a built-in remedy to help us combat whatever anxieties life throws our way: our breath. Simply taking some slow, deep breaths can ease your stress response and activate your relaxation system.

However, if you want to take it up a notch, here are three exercises that you can practice the next time your anxiety needs some quick extra attention.

1. The Held Breath

This is an easy one. You can do it anywhere. Here's how it works:

1. Give your body a quick scan and discover any areas of tension. Once you find them, start counting slowly in your mind: 1, 2...
2. On the count of 4, take a deep, slow breath in. Fill up your lungs fully. Feel your belly rise as you inhale.
3. Hold your breath for at least 8 seconds (or a little longer if you feel comfortable doing that).
4. Purse your lips and exhale slowly while letting the air escape from your mouth. Try to keep exhaling for at least 5 seconds.
5. As you exhale, let go of the tension in your body.

2. The Squeezed Breath

When the sh*t really hits the fan and you need an immediate, fast, powerful release, this exercise can be a good one.

1. Take a very deep breath in and hold it.
2. Tense every muscle in your body as tight as you can for 5 seconds. Squeeze everything! Squeeze your toes, thighs, calves, buttocks,

stomach, chest, arms and hands. Tight! Tight! Tight! The more muscles you squeeze, the better (if you're in a public place though, you can just clench your hands into fists).
3. As you exhale, instantly relax every muscle.
4. Rest for 10 seconds.
5. Repeat this exercise 3 to 5 times. This should take you less than 2 minutes.

If done right, this simple breathing exercise tricks your nervous system into thinking that you've escaped from a threat. You should feel an instant wave of relaxation.

It's helpful to practice both of these exercises a few times over — then you'll have them ready to be pulled out of your back pocket whenever you need it!

3. Go Rag Doll

One of the easiest ways to drop your resistance is to relax your body. If your body relaxes, your mind starts to soften too. There's a quick exercise you can use to do just that.

Have you ever seen one of those old-fashioned, floppy rag dolls? You pick it up and its arms and legs just hang everywhere. I use that metaphor all the time in my yoga class, telling people to go rag doll and let go of resistance. It turns out that it's a nice mental image when it comes to letting go. Just allow your whole body to go rag doll. Drop your shoulders, relax your face, soften that space between your eyebrows and relax your gaze. Just let your muscles hang off your bones.

Why not try it out right now? Relax your body and drop your struggle — even if it's just for a few seconds. See if it brings a little bit of ease into the moment.

WHERE AM I NOW?

So, where am I now? Anxiety has stopped being a problem for me years ago. I often feel like the most relaxed and chilled-out person in the room. Also, everyone else's anxiety seems much more obvious to me.

A few years back, my son had a leukaemia scare. It took a week for us to get his blood report back. The report indicated that he was in the clear, but for the duration of that week, massive fear was my constant companion. As best I could, I softened into and opened up to my fear. I allowed it to exist within me. It was hugely uncomfortable, but that was the truth of my reality at that time. Although it was still a struggle, this acceptance brought a sense of clarity, truth and acknowledgement to the situation. I could cope just a tiny bit better.

When you experience fear that is THAT heavy, you get to know it better. You get familiar with how it feels in your body. And when you face a smaller fear, it really doesn't feel so bad at all.

Recently I sang in public for the first time ever. It really triggered my fight-or-flight response. My body was shaking like a leaf, but my mind was as calm as a Zen monk. The experience was wonderful and fascinating. I thoroughly enjoyed it.

Sometimes I still wonder if there's another me, in a parallel universe of some sort, who has never suffered from anxiety. Sometimes I wonder how that life would have turned out for me. What type of person would I be? I'll never know.

The fact is that I did suffer from anxiety. Massive, crippling anxiety. My experience has permanently shaped me in ways I'll never be able to fully comprehend. Who I am now is, to a large extent, the result of all those years I've spent trapped in the prison of fear.

We're all products of our history. Suffering has been a huge part of my life, and, in truth, it isn't all bad. Suffering gives you knowledge, insight and a deeper understanding of the complexities of our world. Suffering is your experience. It's your wisdom. It's your history. It teaches you what it means to be a human being. Feeling pain gives you a better awareness of other people's pain. It allows you to connect more deeply with other people, to understand them better and to love them more. Everybody's suffering on some level or another, and it is this insight that can help you form some of the most meaningful human connections in your life.

Would I be as passionate about my moment-to-moment experience if I hadn't gone through all of that? Would I have such a deep appreciation for the complexity of human existence? Would I be as keen to empathize with and connect to other people's suffering?

I don't know. I can't tell for sure. But I doubt it.

The best I can do for myself now is to try and acknowledge my history with anxiety. For if I am to be fully me, I must embrace *all* of me. I can't pick and choose which parts of myself to have. I can't choose which parts of myself to love. To love and be grateful for life means to love and be grateful for all of it.

Do I have all the answers? No, of course not. Yet that's the whole point of this book. It's about learning to embrace our vulnerable, sensitive, uncertain side. It's about learning to be okay with not being okay. It's about accepting doubt as a wonderful, integral part of life. In truth, the more I learn, the more I realize how much I don't know.

The only thing I know for certain is that I'm here, in this moment. That's all. I know that I'm sitting in a café, having a nice cup of tea. It's a cloudy, overcast day (it *is* Scotland after all). I know I'm here and I know I'm me, and I know how I feel. Well, sort of. It's complicated beyond words. It feels a bit like energy, like a continuous flow, like excitement, like tingles, like orange, like love, like doubt. It feels like a little bit of everything and, at the same time, nothing much at all.

If I had to label this feeling, I'd say that I feel alive. It's a delicious, tangible sensation of life flowing through my veins. It's the joy of being in the here and now. It's a quiet sort of bliss.

NOW IT'S YOUR TURN

Congratulations! You've made it through. Well done!

I am hopeful I have given you the tools you need to break free from anxiety forever. Now you just need to go forward and apply the Fu*k Fear technique to your life.

Take a moment to imagine yourself one year from now, free from anxiety. Imagine your ideal day. What does it look like? How do you feel? Imagine some of the fun and enjoyable things you'll do once you're no longer stuck in the prison of fear. See yourself handling stressful situations calmly. It feels good, doesn't it?

This *can* be your future. You *can* have hope. So never, ever doubt that you can beat this. You can. You don't have to spend the rest of your life being a slave to your anxiety.

Helping others regain their true selves is my life's passion and it's been an honor to share it with you. Thank you so much for reading *Fu*k Fear* and spending time with me. As best I could, I tried to write this book as a guide to help you break free from fear and rediscover your path towards feeling alive again. Whether or not I succeeded is up to you. But if there's one truth I'm absolutely sure of on this beautiful, rainy day, it's that we only get one life.

You don't have to wait until you're on your deathbed to realize what a waste of your precious life it is to believe that something's wrong with you. Just for a second open yourself up to the possibility that there's nothing wrong with you and there never has been.

Embrace your humanity with all of its marvellous beauty and spectacular flaws. Embrace the imperfect, quirky, beautiful, wonderful person you are. You don't need anyone's approval to embrace yourself. You don't need anyone's acceptance. You don't have to prove yourself worthy because you already are worthy. Fu*k waiting around for the world to tell you that you're good enough. You *are* enough.

Sure, there are hundreds of reasons to play it safe. There are hundreds of reasons to keep on thinking that you're flawed in some fundamental way and that there's nothing you can do about it. Yet you should say, "Fu*k it!" to all of them, open your arms wide and embrace life in all of its glory. Take on the thing you fear. Take on the world, armed with the power of your beautiful heart.

Your life is out there. It's waiting for you. Now fu*k fear and go get it!

THE ONLINE EXPERIENCE

Go deeper with the online experience.

Go to https://ffear.co/ to sign up the online experience.

You will get access to:

- The Fu*k Fear SOS audio (great for when you need a quick fix)
- The Fu*k Fear Guided Meditation - to embed the core ideas of the book into your subconscious.
- My Fu*k Fear Newsletter full of tips and insights.

CAN YOU DO ME A SMALL FAVOR?

This book was born out of my passion for helping people. The problem is that, as companies go, we are very small. *Fu*k Fear* is a self-published book and does not have the marketing resources of a big publishing company.

If, like so many others, you've enjoyed this book, I would greatly appreciate it if you could do me a small (yet big) favor and help me spread the word. That way, we can start a movement and help as many people as possible to overcome their anxiety.

There are two ways you can do this:

1. *Post a tweet or let your Facebook friends know about this book.*

2. *Write an honest review of the book on our Amazon page.* These reviews make a HUGE difference in reassuring others that this book is the real deal.

I'm not looking for anything over the top, unbelievable or fabricated. Instead, I ask for something real and based on what you've read or experienced while reading this book. Also, you can use a pen name or be anonymous when you write an Amazon review.

It's a small favor, but it would make a big difference.

Afterwards, you can reach out to me at richard@ffear.co and let me know how your new, anxiety-free life is progressing!

CONNECT WITH RICHARD KERR

I love being in touch with my readers. You can write to me at richard@ffear.co

Notes

1. My story

1. https://www.cell.com/current-biology/pdfExtended/S0960-9822(16)30174-9

7. Distraction

1. https://www.sciencedaily.com/releases/2018/07/180716164511.htm

18. Day 2: The Fu*k Fear Technique

1. Self-Compassion Induction Reduces Anticipatory Anxiety Among Socially Anxious Students - Elena M. Harwood1 & Nancy L. Kocovski1

23. Day 7: Embrace your humanity

1. https://www.nimh.nih.gov/health/statistics/what-is-prevalence.shtml

www.ingramcontent.com/pod-product-compliance
Lightning Source LLC
Chambersburg PA
CBHW061323040426
42444CB00011B/2746